FUNDAMENTAL TRAINING PRINCIPLES

Essential Knowledge for Building the Elite Athlete

Dr. John R. Mishock

ISBN-10: 1-942489-44-7
ISBN-13: 978-1-942489-44-3

Published by SkillBites Publishing

DEDICATION

To my loving supportive wife Michelle who has stood by my side through our life journeys. To my kids, Ty, Zach, Hunter, and Maddie who are my number one joy in life. I love you all.

INTRODUCTION

This book is designed to educate the coach, health-care provider, trainer, and/or parent on the fundamental training principles and theories that will be used in future Train 2 Play exercise training materials and writings. Understanding these training principals is essential for optimizing youth and adolescent physical development for enhanced sports performance and injury prevention. In today's gym and training world, many exercise programs are sold as "canned" programs with a one-size-fits-all mentality. This type of program can work; however, it is not specific to the young athlete's unique needs. For example, speed and agility programs are commonplace in the exercise training world. These types of programs will be much less effective if the athlete has poor strength of the core or weakness in the legs. In this scenario, strengthening of the core and legs prior to the speed and agility program would be an essential first step in optimizing speed and agility, giving the athlete the best chance for optimal sports performance gains. The more specific the training based on the athlete's unique physical weakness and deficits, the greater the individual improvements. In this book I share the best scientific evidence on body physiology and training principles that when implemented will allow the athlete to optimize training time and efficiency for long-term athletic development.

TRAIN 2 PLAY MISSION STATEMENT

At Train 2 Play, our mission is to provide the most state-of-the-art, scientifically based exercise programs to improve fitness, enhance performance, and minimize or prevent injury.

The primary goal is to arm coaches, parents, fitness professionals, physical educators, and health-care providers with knowledge and practical movement-based exercises that can be done at home to optimize God-given gifts, allowing the athlete to reach peak performance in competition and in life.

TABLE OF CONTENTS

CHAPTER 1

Developing an Athlete for the Long Term: It's More Than a Game!

In the United States, it is estimated that sixty million children and adolescents (aged five to eighteen) play organized sports each year at a cost of over $7 billion and growing.[1] Travel-team parents spend an average of $2,266 annually on their child's sports participation, and at the elite levels some families spend more than $20,000 per year.[2] Many of the parents and coaches of these young athletes approach sports with a "peak by Friday" mentality, expecting instant results in their child's performance. The parents and coaches expect the young athlete to perform at a high level without having committed to the countless hours of training needed for that high level of proficiency.

It has been suggested that it may take eight to twelve years of focused training for a talented athlete to reach the apex of his or her sport. This is also known as the 10,000 hour rule.[3] The exact number of hours is up for debate; however, regardless of the individual's God-given skill, there is a significant amount of time, hard work, and dedication that is required to reach the highest levels of a given sport or activity. Despite the consistent evidence for the value of dedication, hard work, and deliberate practice to reach elite-level status, there is very little evidence for the necessity of deliberate practice during childhood. Research studies comparing elite-level and non-elite-level athletes in a variety of sports have found that training differences did not need to occur until thirteen years of age.[4]

There are specific sports, such as gymnastics, figure skating, dance, and diving, that require early specialization due to peak competitive levels occurring prior to full skeletal maturity. In sports that elite-level performance is reached as an adult, there is no evidence to support that early specialization is needed. There is nothing wrong with specialized training in a given sport at an early age; however, it is important for the parent to recognize that balance is needed between intensive sports participation and other childhood commitments such as friends, school, play, and other extracurricular activities.

It is believed that the overemphasis on immediate results, early specialization in one sport, and the excess amount of competitions or games impedes the young athlete's development of fundamental physical literacy—competence in a wide variety of physical activities in multiple environments that benefits healthy development—and sports-specific skills.[5] The demanding need for instant results in sports puts a significant amount of pressure on the developing child. It is unrealistic for coaches and parents to expect young people to be able to move and make physical plays like adults. These developing children simply do not have the movement-based skill, strength, and coordination to move their bodies like the highly trained elite-level athletes. This lack of proper expectation in coaching, training, and athletic development leads to an inordinate number of kids quitting sports before they even have finished developing physically, mentally, and emotionally. Thus, by age thirteen, 70 percent of kids stop playing sports altogether.[6]

Early sports specialization before the age of thirteen years is associated with increased burnout and sports dropout rates. In a survey of 10,000 youth and adolescents nationwide, it was found that kids stop playing sports because they're not having fun, too much time is required, there's too much pressure, there's too much emphasis on winning, they're developing bad habits due to too much competition, the coach plays favorites, they aren't given enough playing time, they are afraid to make mistakes, and/or they need more time to study.[7]

Most of the coaches in youth sports are volunteers with little or no training. Youth sports organizations are thankful to have volunteers; however, of the two to four million youth coaches, only 20 percent have received any type of training in effective motivational coaching techniques, and just one in three have been trained in skills and tactics in the primary sport they coach.[8] Not to mention the fact that most coaches have little experience in youth and adolescent physical development and exercise training that is relative to the sport they are coaching. The lack of properly trained coaches often leads to an excessive number of competitions or games and an emphasis on sports-specific skills only with little emphasis on developing physical literacy. It is much easier for an untrained coach to have the kids play games versus researching and developing a strong fundamental practice that meets the needs of the child's physical and sports-specific skill development. For example, in basketball it is easier to roll a ball out and just let the kids run around and play versus creating a practice that includes agility and speed drills while working on specific sports-related skills such as dribbling and shooting layups.

Ideally, the coach would develop a practice that covers key components of youth physical development, termed physical literacy. The starting point of physical literacy is the development of the ABCs of youth physical development—agility, balance, coordination, and general body strength. The ABCs are fundamental and an essential foundation for long-term athleticism. In turn, this lack of physical preparation may lead to incomplete athletic development, lending to the epidemic of sports injuries caused by inadequate training and/or overuse.

Physical literacy in children is often negatively affected by parents who have their child specializing in a given sport at too early an age. The definition or criteria for early sports specialization according to Myers and colleges is

- prepubertal (seventh grade or roughly age thirteen years) child;
- participating in year-round specific sport training (greater than eight months per year); and
- choosing a single main sport and/or quitting all other sports to focus on one sport.[9]

Take, for example, a young baseball player whose parents at a young age decide that this is "their" sport. That child plays year-round with the coaches, focusing only on baseball-specific skills. If that young athlete does not participate in other forms of sport or exercise, he or she potentially misses critical windows of physical development in agility, balance, coordination, and strength. Missing developmental milestones from either inactivity or early specialization in a sport can result in overall low strength levels, incorrect landing mechanics, aberrant change-of-direction techniques (inability to control the body while moving quickly), ligamentous laxity (poor supporting ligaments), muscle tightness, nonsymmetrical muscle development (muscles that are developed more on one side of the body), overreliance on a particular limb or movement (excess use of one side of the body during movement), overuse injuries, burnout, and dropping out of all of sports.[10]

Consequently, the child does not develop as an athlete first, potentially leading to the epidemic of sports-related injuries seen in orthopedic and sports physical therapy clinics today. Knee ACL injuries in our soccer players and shoulder or elbow injuries in our baseball players are typical examples. In a study of athletes who met the criteria for early specialization, it was found that the athlete had a 2.25 times greater chance of sustaining a serious overuse injury than an unspecialized young athlete.[11]

In studies looking at elite-level athletes, most report playing multiple sports as a youth and adolescent. For example, 88 percent of Olympians reported participating in more than one sport as a child. In addition, 97 percent of professional athletes believed being a multisport youth athlete was beneficial to their success in becoming elite in their sport.[12]

Research by numerous national governing bodies, including the United States Olympic Committee and many other sports organizations, have proven that early specialization in a sport actually prevents an athlete from reaching his or her full athletic potential and may lead to an inordinate amount of youth and adolescent injuries. The goal should be to develop as an athlete first, playing many sports as a youth before specializing in the late teens when growth plates have closed.[13]

The United States Olympic Committee created the American Development Model in 2014 to help young Americans realize their full athletic potential and utilize sports as a path toward an active and healthy lifestyle. The committee describes five stages of athlete development for optimization of the experience physically, mentally, and emotionally.

- Stage 1: Discover and Play (age 0–12)
- Stage 2: Develop and Challenge (age 10–16)

- Stage 3: Train and Compete (age 13–19)
- Stage 4: Participate and Succeed (age 15+)
- Stage 5: Excel for High Performance (for life)[14]

In stage 1 (age 0–12) the child gets involved with sports at a young age. Programs should encourage the athlete to participate in multiple sports. Coaches are encouraged to allow the child to discover and explore the sport in a fun, enjoyable way. The coaches' main goal should be to inspire the child to enjoy sports through early positive experiences. In this phase, physical literacy is developed through a wide variety of sports experiences, free play (unrestricted movement or activity created and led by children), and general exercise. The child begins to develop psychological and social factors in interpersonal skill, teamwork, and communication. Emphasis is on skill development and sports education versus a large number of games. Seventy percent of the time in the sport should be spent on training and practice while only thirty percent on games or competitions.[15] This is a stark contrast in what we see in America today, with many youth recreational and travel sports organizations having the reverse, 70 percent games to 30 percent practice.

In stage 2 (age 10–16), the athlete has played a sport and shows a genuine interest and motivation in exploring more organized training. This stage focuses on refining the sport-specific skills needed to be successful in the sport. Physically, the young athlete is developing physical literacy in the ABCs of development. The athlete develops interpersonal skills and teamwork while identifying personal strengths and areas in need of improvement.

In stage 3 (age 13–19), training and competition are increased to meet the athlete's interests, goals, and sports development needs. Games and competitions become more important in the development process. Technical, tactical, physical, and psychosocial development becomes increasingly more important for the athlete at this time as they realize the hard work and dedication that it takes to excel. Sport-specific training increases; however, multisport play can continue to be used in order to cross-train for complete athletic development. The emphasis continues to be on practice and skill development over competitions and games.[16] A 60 percent training to 40 percent competition ratio (including both competition and competition-specific training) is recommended through most of this stage.[17]

In stage 4 (age 15+), the athlete reaches high school and there is a crossroad to either play sports at a high-performance, competitive level or to continue to play for the fun, physical health, and social aspects. Growth spurts, experience, hard work, and dedication to training can play a significant role in the athlete's sports career choice. Still at this stage, fun and socialization are key elements to the athlete's desire to continue to play sports.[18]

In stage 5 (for life), there is emphasis on the fact that we all need sports in order to establish physical activity and maintain a healthy lifestyle. Throughout life, many of the previous athletes will give back as coaches, officials, and mentors for their children and other young athletes. For the select few elite athletes, a college or professional career could be had in this stage.[19]

For parents that have their child specialize in a single sport, or if the young athlete participates in intense sports-related training for more hours per week than his or her age (i.e., a seven-year-old spending eight hours a week in a single sport), regardless of the child's age, the parents should take special precautions to assure that the child is developing appropriately physically, mentally, and emotionally. The parents should monitor the child for signs of burnout, overuse injury, and potential negative performance outcomes due to overtraining. The evidence strongly indicates that most youth athletes should be involved in a periodized strength and conditioning program (described later in Train 2 Play writings, which can be found at train2playsports.com) to help the athlete develop appropriate physical literacy in the core areas of strength, balance, coordination, agility, speed, and power. This type of training can be done as part of the sport practices and will help the athlete to prepare for the demands of competitive sport participation.[20] For example, a youth baseball player could perform core exercises as part of his or her warm-up prior to baseball practice. A youth basketball player could perform agility exercises while rehearsing his or her dribbling skill.

Listed below are recommendations for avoiding burnout and overuse injury in youth sports:

- Avoid overscheduling and excessive time commitments.
- Talk to the child regarding his or her desires, wishes, and goals regarding sports.
- Emphasize skill development and fun.
- Emphasize a lifelong passion for physical activity and sports.

But What about My Child's College Scholarship and Professional Career?

As mentioned above, the youth sports circuit is big money, with many of the organizations preying on the parents' and young athlete's dreams of college scholarships and professional careers. There is nothing wrong with the aspiration to play in college or professionally; however, it must be kept in perspective. The chance of a young athlete having a college or professional athletic career in a given sport is minuscule at best. Of the sixty million kids playing youth sports, 25 percent of youth stars become a standout in high school. Only 2–5 percent of high school athletes go on to play college sports. The odds are even smaller to play professionally. The odds of a high school baseball player making it to the MLB is one in four thousand, a high school football player making it to the NFL is one in six thousand, and a high school basketball player making it to the NBA is one in ten thousand.[21]

2016 Estimated Probability of Competing in College Athletics

Men	High School (HS) Participation	NCAA Participation	Overall % HS to NCAA	% HS to NCAA Division I	% HS to NCAA Division II	% HS to NCAA Division III
Baseball	486,567	34,198	7.0%	2.1%	2.2%	2.7%
Basketball	541,479	18,697	3.5%	1.0%	1.0%	1.4%
Football	1,083,617	72,788	6.7%	2.6%	1.8%	2.4%
Soccer	432,569	24,477	5.7%	1.3%	1.5%	2.8%
Golf	148,823	8,654	5.8%	2.0%	1.7%	2.1%
Lacrosse	108,450	13,165	12.1%	2.9%	2.2%	7.1%

Ice Hockey	35,875	4,071	11.3%	4.6%	0.5%	6.3%
Tennis	157,240	8,211	5.2%	1.7%	1.1%	2.4%
Track	578,632	28,177	4.9%	1.9%	1.2%	1.7%
Swimming	137,087	9,715	7.1%	2.8%	1.1%	3.2%
Women						
Basketball	429,504	16,589	3.9%	1.2%	1.1%	1.6%
Field Hockey	60,549	5,894	9.7%	2.9%	1.2%	5.7%
Soccer	375,681	26,995	7.2%	2.4%	1.9%	2.9%
Golf	72,582	5,221	7.2%	3.0%	2.1%	2.1%
Lacrosse	84,785	10,994	13.0%	3.7%	2.5%	6.7%
Ice Hockey	9,418	2,175	23.1%	9.0%	1.1%	13.1%
Tennis	182,876	8,960	4.9%	1.6%	1.1%	2.2%
Track	478,726	28,797	6.0%	2.7%	1.5%	1.8%
Swimming	166,838	12,428	3.9%	1.2%	1.2%	1.6%

Adapted from http://www.ncaa.org/about/resources/research/estimated-probability-competing-professional-athletics.

2016 Estimated Probability of Competing in Professional Sports

	NCAA Participants	Approximate # Draft Eligible	# Draft Picks	# NCAA Drafted	% NCAA to Major Pro	% NCAA to Total Pro
Football	72,788	16,175	356	256	1.6%	1.9%
Men's Basketball	18,697	4,155	60	46	1.1%	12.2%
Women's Basketball	16,589	3,686	36	36	0.9%	4.7%
Baseball	34,198	7,600	1,215	738	9.7%	-
Ice Hockey	4,071	905	210	60	6.6%	-
Men's Soccer	24,447	5,439	75	75	1.4%	-

Adapted from http://www.ncaa.org/about/resources/research/estimated-probability-competing-professional-athletics.

Despite the limited odds of having a high school, college, or even pro sports career, participation in sports and exercise is associated with a range of documented physical, emotional, social, educational, and other benefits that can last a lifetime.

How Important Is It for Young People to Participate in Exercise and Sports?

When children don't exercise or play sports, they have impaired physical literacy and improper movement pattern development, which often leads to a diminished interest in any type of physical activity and free play. Free play or pick-up games and activities promote innovation and high levels of fitness. Free play was commonplace in previous generations but is now being replaced with screens and electronic devices (mobile phones, computers, video games, and TV) or adult-organized sports. More than one in three parents say it is a challenge to make sure their children get enough exercise each week.[22] Devoid of sports, exercise, and free play, by age nine, physical activity rates begin to drop sharply in those individuals who are not regularly physically active. By age fifteen, moderate to vigorous physical activity declines by 75 percent, with less than forty minutes per weekday and thirty minutes per weekend. Among youth six to seventeen years of age, one in five report having no physical activity at all.[23] A sedentary lifestyle can then follow. It is well documented that sedentary living causes such health problems as obesity, diabetes, high blood pressure, cardiovascular disease, and other chronic diseases. These can begin in childhood and evolve to form a lifelong problem. In recent years, the childhood obesity rate has nearly tripled. The percentage of children aged six to eleven who are classified as obese has increased from 7 percent in 1980 to 17.5 percent in 2014; among children aged twelve to nineteen, that figure has grown from 5 percent to 20.5 percent. One in three children today is obese or overweight.[24] If all 12.7 million US youth with obesity become obese adults, the societal costs over their lifetimes for health care and other related costs may exceed $1.1 trillion.[25]

Early sports participation and formal exercise can be a countermeasure to a sedentary lifestyle, which is clearly prevalent and dangerous. Regular physical activity and exercise benefits children in many ways, including building and maintaining healthy bones, strengthening muscles, improving cardiovascular fitness, controlling body weight, and preventing or delaying the development of high blood pressure and other diseases such as cardiovascular disease, diabetes, and some cancers.[26] For example, a comprehensive study found that leisure-time physical activity and exercise is associated with reduced risk of thirteen different types of cancer, including breast, colon, liver, and leukemia.[27]

Exercise and Sports…More Than Physical Health

Sports participation and exercise has been shown to lead to enhanced concentration, improved grades, and higher standardized test scores. It can help in personal development by improving self-esteem, increasing confidence, establishing proper goal setting, and enhancing leadership skills.[28]

Playing sports is often thought of as a metaphor for life, creating opportunities to learn life lessons in a nurturing environment. Learning commitment, dedication, and hard work along with how to deal with winning, losing, and individual failure are basic tenants found in sports. With that, high school athletes are more likely than nonathletes to attend college and get degrees.[29] In the workplace, a survey of four hundred female corporate executives found that 94 percent played a sport. Of those women, 61 percent said that the lessons learned from the sport contributed to their career success.[30]

Beyond the psychosocial and health benefits of exercise is the financial savings to our global economy. An active lifestyle could save nearly $68 billion annually in medical costs and another $28 billion in lost work productivity in the US. Thirty minutes of exercise just five times per week could save more than $2,500 per person in health-care-related savings.[31]

Ultimately, youth sports participation and exercise should be fun and inspiring, leading to a lifelong passion for physical activity and fitness. Adolescents who play sports are eight times as likely to be active at age twenty-four.[32] Three in four (77 percent of) adults aged thirty and above who play sports today played sports as school-aged children. Only 3 percent of all adults who play sports currently did not play when they were young.[33]

The Train 2 Play sports writings are scientifically based to help coaches, teachers, parents, trainers, and health-care providers teach proper physical literacy and improve athleticism through basic movement patterns, progressing to advanced exercise and training techniques. First, the young athlete develops his or her relative maximum strength, which is maximum strength specific to efficient body movements. Once the child or adolescent has the base of relative maximum strength developed, exercises can be progressed to improve balance, coordination, agility, power, explosiveness, and acceleration/deceleration change of direction. For example, a young athlete may not be able to hold a side plank for sixty seconds or do ten good push-ups. In this case the athlete would want to develop strength in those activities prior to beginning a plyometric medicine ball routine. In doing so he or she would have built a good foundation of body strength that could be used for sports-specific exercise training. The ultimate goal is to develop an athlete first who has the foundation to acquire any sports-specific skill.

The development of the young athlete's physical body in a scientific way will lead to improved sports performance, allowing the athlete to optimally express his or her God-given genetics and skill. The Train 2 Play approach potentially makes the athlete less susceptible to injury. Ultimately, this training program will hopefully create a lifelong passion for exercise and movement to maintain health and prevent disease.

References

1 Minnesota Amateur Sports Commission, Athletic Footwear Association, *USA Today* Survey, Michigan State, 2012.

2 Mike Sagas and George Cunningham, preparers, "Sport Participation Rates among Underserved American Youth," University of Florida's Sport Policy & Research Collaborative (2014).

3 K. Anders Ericsson, Ralf Th. Krampe, and Clemens Tesch-Romer, "The Role of Deliberate Practice in the Acquisition of Expert Performance," *Psychological Review* 100 (1993): 363–406.

4 Ibid.; Werner F.Helsen, Janet L. Starkes, and Nicola J. Hodges, "Team Sports and the Theory of Deliberate Practice," *Journal of Sport and Exercise Psychology* 20 (1998): 12–3; Joseph Baker, Janice Deakin, and Jean Côté, "Expertise in Ultra-Endurance Triathletes: Early Sport Involvement, Training Structure, and the Theory of Deliberate Practice," *Journal of Applied Sport Psychology* 17 (2005): 64–78.

5 Istvan Balyi, "Long-Term Athlete Development: The System and Solutions," 2001, http://www.oxspa.co.uk/uploads/long-term-athlete-development-article.pdf.

6 Amanda J. Visek et al., "The Fun Integration Theory: Towards Sustaining Children and Adolescents Sport Participation," *Journal of Physical Activity & Health* 12 no. 3 (2014): 424–433.

7 Ibid.

8 Aspen Institute Sports & Society Program by the Sports & Fitness Industry Association, 2013.

9 G. D. Myer et al., "Sports Specialization, Part I: Does Early Sports Specialization Increase Negative Outcomes and Reduce the Opportunity for Success in Young Athletes?" *Sports Health* 7 no. 5 (2015): 437–442.

10 Ibid.; G. D. Myer et al., "Sports Specialization, Part II: Alternative Solutions to Early Sport Specialization in Youth Athletes," *Sports Health* 8 no. 1 (Jan-Feb 2016): 65–73.

11 Neeru A. Jayanthi et al., "Sports-Specialized Intensive Training and the Risk of Injury in Young Athletes: A Clinical Case-Control Study," *American Journal of Sports Medicine* 43 no. 4 (2015): 794–801.

12 Robert F. LaPrade et al., "AOSSM Early Sport Specialization Consensus Statement," *Orthopaedic Journal of Sports Medicine* 4 no. 4 (Apr 2016). doi: 2325967116644241.

13 "The American Development Model," Team USA, 2017. http://www.teamusa.org/About-the-USOC/Athlete-Development/American-Development-Model.

14 LaPrade, "AOSSM Early Sport Specialization Consensus Statement."

15 "The American Development Model."

16 Jayanthi, "Sports-Specialized Intensive Training."

17 Istvan Balyi, Richard Way, and Colin Higgs, *Long-Term Athlete Development*. (Champaign, IL: Human Kinetics, 2016): 150.

18 "The American Development Model."

19 Ibid.

20 Jayanthi, "Sports-Specialized Intensive Training."

21 Scholarship stats, 2015. http://scholarshipstats.com; "Estimated Probability of Competing in Professional Athletics," NCAA, last updated March 10, 2017. http://www.ncaa.org/about/resources/research/estimated-probability-competing-professional-athletics.

22 RWJF/Harvard School of Public Health, 2016.

23 Balyi, *Long-Term Athlete Development*.

24 Philip Nader et al., "Moderate-to-Vigorous Physical Activity From Ages 9 to 15 Years," *JAMA* 300 no. 3 (2008): 295–305; "Childhood Overweight and Obesity," Centers for Disease Control and Prevention, 2015 https://www.cdc.gov/obesity/childhood/.

25 Fred Dews, "Societal Cost of Obesity Could Exceed $1.1 Trillion, New Brookings Research Finds," Brookings, 2015. https://www.brookings.edu/blog/brookings-now/2015/05/12/societal-cost-of-obesity-could-exceed-1-1-trillion-new-brookings-research-finds/.

26 NIH Research Matters, "Physical Activity Associated with Lower Risk of Many Cancers," National Institutes of Health, 2016. https://www.nih.gov/news-events/nih-research-matters/physical-activity-associated-lower-risk-many-cancers.

27 "Facts: Sports Activity and Children," Aspen Institute Project Play, 2016. https://www.aspenprojectplay.org/the-facts.

28 US Dept. of Education, 2005. http://instructional1.calstatela.edu/dfrankl/curr/kin385/pdf/hs-athletics-stats-05.pdf

29 Ibid.; EY. "Female Executives Say Participation in Sport Helps Accelerate Leadership and Career Potential." London, 10 October 2014. http://www.ey.com/gl/en/newsroom/news-releases/news-female-executives-say-participation-in-sport-helps-accelerate--leadership-and-career-potential.

30 EY. "Female Executives."

31 *The Lancet* Physical Activity Series. Physical Activity: Progress and Challenges. The Lancet (27 July 2016).. http://www.thelancet.com/series/physical-activity-2016.

32 Daniel F. Perkins et al., "Childhood and Adolescent Sports Participation as Predictors of Participation in Sports and Physical Fitness Activities in Young Adulthood," *SAGE Journals* 35 no. 4 (2004).

33 Sports and Health In America. NPR. Robert Wood Johnson Foundation. Harvard T.H. Chan School of Public Health. June 2015. http://media.npr.org/documents/2015/june/sportsandhealthpoll.pdf

CHAPTER 2

Youth and Adolescent Exercise Training: Fact or Fiction

For our purpose, "youth" will be defined as six to eleven years old. "Adolescent" will be defined as twelve to eighteen years old. These definitions apply to both males and females. The challenge with growing children is that at any given chronological age (the number of years alive), there can be up to four years difference biologically (the estimated age of your body based on physical development and maturity) in either direction. In other words, two ten-year-old children chronologically could differ from one another by up to eight years biologically, making one six years old and the other fourteen years old physically. It is not known why some children and adolescents mature at different rates; however, it is certainly an early advantage in youth and adolescent sports. For example, take any sixth or seventh grade sports team and you will see an athlete approaching six feet tall with masculine features and another adolescent who is a foot smaller, looking like they belong in grade school. With this, it is imperative for the trainer or parent to understand the individual child's physical, mental, and emotional maturity and tailor the exercise program to the young athlete's individual needs.

In this chapter I will review the commonly held myths about the safety of youth and adolescent exercise. Many of these beliefs have been handed down from generation to generation. Today, more than ever, there is an abundance of scientific studies debunking these beliefs.

Ultimately, I want you to understand that exercise is safe when certain safety guidelines are followed.

Is Exercise Training Unsafe for Children?

Exercise training is defined as physical exercise that uses body weight or resistance to induce the development of the muscular system. Plyometric training is a type of exercise in which muscles exert maximum force in short intervals of time. (This will be described in great detail later in the book.) Youth plyometric and resistance training, as with most physical activities, does carry some degree of inherent risk of muscle, ligament, or bone injury, yet this risk is no greater than many other sports and recreational activities in which children and adolescents regularly participate. In a prospective study that evaluated the incidence of sports-related injuries in school-aged youth over a one-year period, resistance training resulted in less injury individually than football, basketball, and soccer. In the 1,576 injuries documented, 0.7 percent occurred during exercise training, while 19 percent were from football, 15 percent from basketball, and 2 percent from soccer.[1]

In a number of youth exercise injury studies, it was found that most injuries were due to aggressive progression of training loads or improper exercise technique, not the exercises themselves.[2] With appropriate supervision and sensible progression of exercise intensity and volume, the risk of injury is no greater than a child's normal physical activity and play. The key is to follow strict safety guidelines and precautions.

The Train 2 Play exercise programs use a comprehensive training approach to develop and optimize the human body's athletic potential through the use of exercise training and plyometrics.

Should You Wait to Perform Resistance or Plyometric Training until You Have Reached Puberty?

Children and adolescents can begin exercise training when they have the emotional maturity to accept and follow directions, as early as six to eight years of age. Reaching puberty does not give the athlete any more advantage to safety versus prepubescent youth.[3]

Will Children Experience Bone and Growth Plate Damage with Plyometric or Resistance Training?

In the growing bone, there are three main sites of growth: the growth plates near the ends of the long bones, the cartilage lining the joint surfaces (articular cartilage), and the points at which the major tendons attach to the bones (apophysis). The theory was that growth cartilage is "pre-bone" and is weaker than adjacent connective tissue and therefore more easily damaged by repetitive microtrauma (small cellular breakdown) from exercise training. Conversely, it has been found that adolescent growing cartilage may actually be stronger and more resistant to shearing-type forces than that of adults.[4] Furthermore, research supports the fact that growth plate injuries are actually less in children performing an exercise routine versus children not exercising at all. Furthermore, the growth plates actually become stronger with the physical stress, preventing or minimizing shear-related injuries of the growth plate.[5]

The bottom line is that injury to the growth cartilage has not been reported in any prospective youth exercise training research study. There is no evidence to suggest that resistance training will negatively impact growth and maturation during childhood or adolescence.[6]

Is Plyometric Training Only for Young Athletes Playing Sports?

Plyometric exercises typically include hops, jumps, throws, and other explosive movements that exploit the muscles' stretch-shortening cycle, which increases muscle power. If one watches children on a playground, skips, jumps, and pulls are similar to plyometric training. This type of exercise, although often game-like in nature, actually conditions the body to increase speed of movement and improve power production.[7]

Children of all abilities can benefit from resistance and plyometric training. Regular participation in this type of training can lead to enhanced physical fitness, minimizing the deleterious effects of a sedentary lifestyle in boys and girls.[8]

In a systematic review of children five to fourteen years old performing plyometric training, it was suggested that plyometric training is safe for children of all abilities, whether an athlete or not, provided there is appropriate skilled supervision, children who have agreed to participate, and safety guidelines built into the intervention.[9]

Can Resistance and Plyometric Training Cause Muscle and Other Soft-Tissue Injuries?

Like with any physical activity, there is the potential for injury to occur if the intensity, volume, or frequency of training exceeds the physiological abilities of the participants. This type of overtraining can potentially create soft-tissue (muscle or ligament) injury.

In several reports, lower back pain was the most frequent injury in high school athletes who participated in aggressive resistance training programs beyond the athlete's physical limits.[10] Another study showed that adolescent powerlifters, who train at maximal or near-maximal resistances, increase their likelihood of lower back pain.[11] On the other hand, insufficient strength, muscular endurance, and stability in the lower back have been associated with current and future lower back pain in adolescents.[12]

In the Train 2 Play method, the exercise programs are designed to create strength relative to the adolescent's own body weight (relative maximum strength) using appropriate and safe resistance. Powerlifting is not part of the Train 2 Play method. In the Train 2 Play method, we would expect a reduced prevalence of lower back pain and other musculoskeletal injuries. Furthermore, the risk of injury with training can be dramatically reduced with qualified supervision, appropriate program design, and sensible progression of the exercises.

Based on the evidence, there is no justifiable safety reason that would preclude children or adolescents from participating in plyometric or resistance training programs. Prior to starting an exercise program, consultation with a physician or health-care provider is advised to assure readiness for training.

Can Children Improve Athleticism or Sports Performance through Exercise?

A compelling body of scientific evidence demonstrates that children and adolescents can significantly increase their speed, endurance, strength, agility, quickness, and power above and beyond what growth and maturation will give them with proper exercise and training.[13]

Studies involving basketball, swimming, ice hockey, baseball, and soccer have noted the importance of incorporating resistance exercise into sports training to maximize gains in strength and power in young athletes. Numerous authors have shown that a well-designed, sports-specific training program including resistance and plyometric training, speed, and agility can result in improvements in athletic development and performance.[14] Increases in long jump, vertical jump, sprint speed, and medicine ball toss have been observed in children and adolescents after resistance training with weight machines, free weights, body weight strength exercises, and medicine ball routines.[15]

Further improving the potential for athleticism was the finding that a combination of resistance and plyometric training can give greater benefits than when each is done alone.[16] In the Train 2 Play method, we use the scientific evidence of the synergy of resistance and plyometric training in a functional, sports-specific manner to create optimal athleticism.

There has been a lot of debate on how much prepubescent athletes can improve in strength and endurance due in part to the fact that they do not have an abundance of hormones such as testosterone or growth hormone in their systems. However, one study demonstrated 74 percent improvements in strength gains after eight weeks of a progressive resistance training program.[17] This type of gain may not be typical, but most studies indicate that the young athlete should gain up to 30 percent in strength, endurance, speed, and power after a short-term (eight- to twenty-week) youth training program.[18]

Does Exercise Help to Prevent Sports-Related Injury?

In our world today, athletes are playing more sports than ever; games all year round, multiple sports teams, inadequate rest periods in season and between seasons, and early sports specialization have led to an inordinate amount of sports-related injuries.[19] Many of these injuries are related to ill-prepared or improperly trained young athletes.[20]

Being less physically active overall often leads to a lack of relative maximum strength. This lack of base strength in adolescents creates a poor foundation for future athletic development. Core, upper, and lower body strength is an essential base to build dynamic balance, power, speed, agility, and quickness. In many situations, the young athlete is not prepared physically for the demands of sports practice and competition.[21] Couple this with the excessive amount of seasons and games and it may lead to the epidemic that we see in orthopedic physical therapy clinics today. These injuries in youth sports are a significant financial cost to the health-care system. Beyond this, they often cause athletes to drop out of sports and physical activity altogether.[22]

The total elimination of sports-related injuries is unrealistic; however, an appropriately designed exercise program that includes resistance and plyometric training may help reduce the likelihood of sports-related injuries in both young and adult athletes.[23] In a few studies, it has been suggested that if the athlete is trained appropriately through conditioning, strengthening, muscle imbalances correction, and training errors correction, up to 50 percent of injuries could be reduced.[24]

Based on the evidence, a comprehensive conditioning program that includes resistance, speed, balance, and plyometric training has been shown to be an essential strategy for reducing the epidemic of sports-related injuries in our young athletes.[25]

References

1 B. Zaricznyj et al., "Sports-Related Injuries in School-Aged Children," *American Journal of Sports Medicine* 8 no. 5 (1980): 318–324.

2 James R. Ryan and Gino G. Salciccioli, "Fractures of the Distal Radial Epiphysis in Adolescent Weight Lifters," *American Journal of Sports Medicine* 4 no. 1 (1976): 26–27; Vincent L. Gumbs et al., "Bilateral Distal Radius and Ulnar Fractures in Adolescent Weight Lifters." *American Journal of Sports Medicine* 10 no. 6 (1982): 375–379; Eugene W. Brown and Richard G. Kimball, "Medical History Associated with Adolescent Powerlifting," *Pediatrics* 72 no. 5 (1983).

3 Thomas A. Brady, Bernard R. Cahill, B, and Leslie M. Bodnar, "Weight Training-Related Injuries in the High School Athlete." *American Journal of Sports Medicine* 10 no. 1 (1982): 1–5.

4 Lyle Micheli, "Strength Training in the Young Athlete," in *Competitive Sports for Children and Youth*, ed. Eugene Brown and Crystal Branta (Champaign, IL: Human Kinetics, 1988), 99–105; Lyle Micheli, "Preventing Injuries in Sports: What the Team Physician Needs to Know," in *F.I.M.S. Team Physician Manual*, 2nd ed., eds. K. Chan et al., (Hong Kong: CD Concept, 2006), 555–572.

5 Lyle Micheli, "Strength Training in the Young Athlete," *NSCA's Performance Training Journal*. www.nsca-lift.org/perform.

6 Robert M. Malina, "Weight Training in Youth-Growth, Maturation and Safety: An Evidenced-Based Review," *Clinical Journal of Sports Medicine* 16 no. 6 (2006): 478–487; Steven J. Fleck and William J. Kraemer, *Designing Resistance Training Programs* 3rd ed. (Champaign, IL: Human Kinetics, 2004).

7 Donald A. Chu, Avery D. Faigenbaum, and Jeff E. Falkel, *Progressive Plyometrics for Kids* (Monterey, CA: Healthy Learning, 2006).

8 Avery D. Faigenbaum, "Strength Training for Children and Adolescents," *Clinics in Sports Medicine* 19 no. 4 (October 2000): 593–619.

9 Barbara A. Johnson, Charles L. Salzberg, and David A. Stevenson, "A Systematic Review: Plyometric Training Programs for Young Children," *Journal of Strength and Conditioning Research* 25 no. 9 (2011): 2623–2633.

10 William L. Risser, Jan M. Risser, J, and D. Preston, "Weight-Training Injuries in Adolescents," *American Journal of Diseases in Children* 144 (1990): 1015–1017.

11 Brown, "Medical History Associated with Adolescent Powerlifting."

12 Soares, "Children Are Less Susceptible to Exercise-Induced Muscle Damage than Adults."

13 C. Blimkie et al., "Effects of Resistance Training on Bone Mineral Content and Density in Adolescent Females," *Canadian Journal of Physiology and*

Pharmacology 74 (1996): 1025–1033; C. DeRenne et al., "Effects of Training Frequency on Strength Maintenance in Pubescent Baseball Players," *Journal of Strength and Conditioning Research* 10 (1996): 8–14; Avery D. Faigenbaum et al., "The Effects of Different Resistance Training Protocols on Upper Body Strength and Endurance Development in Children," *Journal of Strength and Conditioning Research* 15 no. 4 (2001): 459–465; Avery D. Faigenbaum and Patrick Mediate, "The Effects of Medicine Ball Training on Physical Fitness in High School Physical Education Students," *Physical Educator* 63 (2006): 160–167; W. Lillegard et al., "Efficacy of Strength Training in Prepubescent to Early Postpubescent Males and Females: Effects of Gender and Maturity," *Pediatric Rehabilitation* 1 (1997): 147–157; Matthew Pikosky et al., "Effects of Resistance Training on Protein Utilization in Healthy Children," *Medicine and Science in Sports and Exercise* 34 (2002): 820–827; David Szymanski et al., "Effect of Twelve Weeks of Medicine Ball Training on High School Baseball Players," *Journal of Strength and Conditioning Research* 21 (2007): 894–901; Charilaos Tsolakis, George Vagenas, and Athanasois Dessypris, "Strength Adaptations and Hormonal Responses to Resistance Training and Detraining in Preadolescent Males," *Journal of Strength and Conditioning Research* 18 (2004): 625–629; W. Westcott, J. Tolken, and B. Wessner, "School-Based Conditioning Programs for Physically Unfit Children," *Strength and Conditioning Journal* 17 (1995): 5–9..

14 E. Vamvakoudis et al., "Effects of Basketball Training on Maximal Oxygen Uptake, Muscle Strength, and Joint Mobility in Young Basketball Players," *Journal of Strength and Conditioning Research* 21 (2007): 930–936; M. Christou et al., "Effects of Resistance Training on the Physical Capacities of Adolescent Soccer Players," *Journal of Strength and Conditioning Research* 20 (2006): 783–791; Lyle Micheli and Laura Purcell, eds., *The Adolescent Athlete: A Practical Approach* (New York: Springer, 2007); William J. Kraemer and Steven Fleck, *Strength Training for Young Athletes*, 2nd ed. (Champaign, IL: Human Kinetics, 2005); Avery D. Faigenbaum and Wayne Westcott, *Youth Strength Training for Health, Fitness and Sport*. (Champaign, IL: Human Kinetics, 2009).

15 W. Weltman et al., "The Effects of Hydraulic Resistance Strength Training in Pre-pubertal Males," *Medicine and Science in Sports and Exercise* 18 (1986): 629–638; Szymanski et al., "Effect of Twelve Weeks of Medicine Ball Training."; Lillegard et al., "Efficacy of Strength Training in Prepubescent to Early Postpubescent Males and Females."; R. Hetzler et al., "Effects of 12 Weeks of Strength Training on Anaerobic Power in Prepubescent Male Athletes," *Journal of Strength and Conditioning Research* 11 (1997): 174–181; S. Flanagan et al., "Effects of Two Different Strength Training Modes on Motor Performance in Children," *Research Quarterly for Exercise and Sport* 73 (2002): 340–344.

16 Eduardo Santos and Manuel Janeira, "Effects of Complex Training on Explosive Strength in Adolescent Male Basketball Players," *Journal of Strength and*

Conditioning Research 22 (2008): 903–909; G. D. Myer et al., "Neuromuscular Training Improves Performance and Lower Extremity Biomechanics in Female Athletes," *Journal of Strength and Conditioning Research* 19 (2005): 51–60.

17 Avery D. Faigenbaum et al., "Preliminary Evaluation of an After-School Resistance Training Program," *Perceptual and Motor Skills* 104 (2007): 407–415.

18 Lillegard et al., "Efficacy of Strength Training in Prepubescent to Early Postpubescent Males and Females."; R. Pfeiffer and R. Francis, "Effects of Strength Training on Muscle Development in Prepubescent, Pubescent and Postpubescent males," *Physician and Sportsmedicine* 14 (1986): 134–143; N. Wedderkopp et al., "Comparison of Two Intervention Programmes in Young Female Players in European Handball: With and Without Ankle Disc," *Scandinavian Journal of Medicine and Science in Sports* 13 (2003): 371–375.

19 Lyle Micheli, Rita Glassman, and Michelle Klein, "The Prevention of Sports Injuries in Youth," *Clinics in Sports Medicine* 19 (2000): 821–834; Carolyn A. Emery, Willem H. Meeuwisse, and Jenelle R. McAllister, "Survey of Sport Participation and Sport Injury Risk in Calgary and Area High Schools," *Clinical Journal of Sports Medicine* 16 (2006): 20–26.

20 D. Caine, C. Caine, and N. Maffulli, "Incidence and Distribution of Pediatric Sport-Related Injuries," *Clinical Journal of Sports Medicine* 16 (2006): 500–513.

21 Micheli, Glassman, and Klein, "The Prevention of Sports Injuries in Youth."; Emery, Meeuwisse, and McAllister, "Survey of Sport Participation."

22 Karen Grimmer, Denise Jones, and Jenny Williams, "Prevalence of Adolescent Injury from Recreational Exercise: An Australian Perspective," *Journal of Adolescent Health* 27 (2000): 266–272.

23 A. Smith, J. Andrish, and L. Micheli, "The Prevention of Sports Injuries in Children and Adolescents," *Medicine and Science in Sports and Exercise* 25 (1993): S1–S8; Micheli, Glassman, and Klein, "The Prevention of Sports Injuries in Youth."; T. Hewett, G. D. Myer, and K. Ford, "Reducing Knee and Anterior Cruciate Ligament Injuries among Female Athletes," *Journal of Knee Surgery* 18 (2005): 82–88; Liz Abernethy and Chris Bleakley, "Strategies to Prevent Injury in Adolescent Sport: A Systematic Review," *British Journal of Sports Medicine* 41 (2007): 627–638.

24 Micheli, "Preventing Injuries in Sports."

25 Odd-Egil Olsen et al., "Exercises to Prevent Lower Limb Injuries in Youth Sports: Cluster Randomized Controlled Trial," *British Medical Journal* 330 (2005): 449; Bert Mandelbaum et al., "Effectiveness of a Neuromuscular and Proprioceptive Training Program in Preventing Anterior Cruciate Ligament Injuries in Female Athletes," *American Journal of Sports Medicine* 33 (2005): 1003–1010; T. Hewett, et al., "The Effects of Neuromuscular Training on the Incidence of Knee Injury in Female Athletes: A Prospective Study," *American*

Journal of Sports Medicine 27 (1999): 699–706; Robert S. Heidt et al., "Avoidance of Soccer Injuries with Preseason Conditioning," *American Journal of Sports Medicine* 28 (2000): 659–662; Jeppe Bo Lauerson, Ditte Marie Bertelsen, and Lars Bo Andersen,, "The Effectiveness of Exercise Interventions to Prevent Sports Injuries," *British Journal of Sports Medicine* 48 (2014): 871–877.

CHAPTER 3

The Physiology of Youth and Adolescent Exercise

When children and early adolescents see gains in parameters involving strength and speed, it appears that those changes have strong neurological mechanisms (i.e., increased motor unit activation and changes in motor unit coordination, recruitment, and firing; motor skill development) rather than hypertrophic (increased muscle mass and girth) factors.[1] In other words, with exercise training, the young athlete will not build significant amounts of muscle mass like a powerlifter or bodybuilder. However, they can see some gains in strength and speed secondary to a nerve- and muscle-learning affect. In later adolescence, during puberty, hormones (testosterone, growth hormone, and insulin-like growth factor) are secreted, allowing males to see considerable increases in muscle mass and linear growth.[2] This is where significant gains in strength and speed can be had. Training-induced strength gains during and after puberty in males may therefore be associated with changes due to hormonal influences on the muscle. In females there are smaller amounts of testosterone, thus limiting the magnitude of training-induced increases in muscle hypertrophy.[3]

Energy Systems Used in Sports and Training

When training athletes, it's important to understand the energy systems utilized to optimize the exercise routine for enhanced sports performance. The ability of the body to produce energy is a fundamental aspect of life. Without the adequate production of energy, the success of the athlete would be in jeopardy. Energy is needed in every cell in the body for basic function and to produce optimal sports performance. The muscle, heart, lungs, brain, and other organs rely on the optimization of the energy systems. For example, significant amounts of energy are required for the brain to coordinate the intricate firing of hundreds of muscles in fractions of a second to create specific movements for athletic activity. Those muscles need adequate energy to move the body in dynamic and diverse ways. Efficient, highly functioning energy systems are the basis for elite athletic performance.

There are three systems used by the body for energy during all functions of the body, known as the aerobic-anaerobic continuum. They are the anaerobic/ATP-PC system, lactic acid system, and aerobic system.[4] I will focus on this system as it relates to training and sports-related activities.

- **Anaerobic/ATP-PC system** is used in explosive activities and sports, requiring eight to ten seconds of maximum output. Sprinters, jumpers, football players, and weightlifters all preferentially use this system.
- **Lactic acid system** is for events of slightly longer duration, up to about forty seconds. The two-hundred-meter and four-hundred-meter runs in track, speed skating, and some gymnastic events utilize this system.
- **Aerobic system** is utilized for sports lasting anywhere from two to three minutes to several hours. Examples of these include cross country running and cross country skiing.

In most sports, we use all three energy systems at any given time. Many sports use a combination of systems during play, such as soccer, basketball, baseball, lacrosse, and volleyball, just to name a few. Understanding the energy utilized in the sport and creating a program that replicates the sports-related activity is integral for elite training. Researchers have found that the closer an athlete trains to the physiological demands of the sport, the greater his or her ability to perform at high levels with superior skill under fatigue. (This is based on the SAID principle, which will be discussed in chapter 5). With this in mind, combining game-specific skill training with physical conditioning leads to optimal transfer relative to game performance. The training routine must consider the energy needs for recovery following the competition or training. The exercise routine should mimic the work-to-rest ratio in the given sport.[5] For example, in football the average play may run seven to ten seconds with roughly twenty to sixty seconds of recovery. The players are mainly using the anaerobic/ATP-PC system and the aerobic system. So when developing a training program, it is important to mimic the work cycle of seven to ten seconds with the rest cycle of twenty to sixty seconds.

Another example is the NCAA division 1 men's basketball game. A starting player averages 34.5 minutes of total playing time per game. He takes part in eight series per half, each about 2.5 minutes long and consisting of nineteen to twenty-two intermittent work bouts. The average duration of these bouts is eight to nine seconds, with none exceeding twenty seconds. Forty-seven percent of the bouts involve high-intensity effort, with the remainder performed at submaximal effort levels. During each series there is usually one short recovery interval (twenty-five to forty seconds long) every eleven bouts. There is a longer (fifty-second to two-minute) time-out every nineteen bouts.[6] So in this case, specific skill and conditioning training may involve twenty-two full-court shuttle runs while dribbling a basketball, each taking nine seconds to complete. Within the shuttle run, props (cones, agility ladders, or agility poles) could be utilized to mimic defenders, which the player must navigate while dribbling. Between repetitions, the player would be allowed fifteen seconds to jog to the baseline while dribbling with his or her weak hand to line up for the next repetition. After the eleventh shuttle run, there would be a twenty-five- to forty-second break in which the individual would perform chest passes against the wall. There would be a fifty-second to two-minute break after the nineteenth set. This is an example of how a basketball coach or trainer could use all three energy systems during training while enhancing conditioning and basketball-specific skill.

In summary, being as specific to the demands of the sport based on the energy systems utilized will help prepare the athlete for the energy demands during competition, minimizing fatigue and improving sports performance. When the energy system is challenged appropriately, there will be a training effect leading to increased athletic performance. If the energy is not supplied fast enough, there will be a reduction in force, power, and performance. In most sports, energy is needed for a specific period of time. If the energy system is not efficient and economical, the individual will run out of energy, leading to altered performance. Lastly, the athlete needs to be able to recover quickly following bursts of activity. In first understanding the energy demands of the sport, a training program can be developed specifically to cause positive adaptations in the nervous system and cardiovascular system to meet the athlete's demands.

The Predominant Energy System for the Selected Sports (By Percent Used)

Sport	Anaerobic/ATP-PC System	Lactic Acid System	Aerobic System
100-meter sprint	98	2	-
50-meter swim	95	5	-
Football	90	10	-
Gymnastics	90	10	-
Volleyball	90	10	-
Baseball	80	15	5
100-meter swim	80	15	5
Basketball	80	10	10
Soccer backs, strikers	80	20	-
Ice hockey forward/defense	80	20	-
Tennis (singles)	70	20	10
Field hockey	60	20	20
Soccer midfielders	60	20	20
Wrestling	45	55	-
Rowing	20	30	70
1,500-meter swim	10	20	70
800-meter sprint	10	60	30
1,500-meter run	5	35	60

Adapted from Scott Powers and Edward Howley, *Exercise Physiology: Theory and Application to Fitness and Performance* 4th ed. (Boston: McGraw Hill, 2001).

References

1 D. Sale, "Strength Training in Children," in *Perspectives in Exercise Science and Sports Medicine*, eds. G. Gisolfi and D Lamb (Indianapolis, IN: Benchmark Press, 1989), 165–216; J. A. Ramsay et al., "Strength Training Effects in Prepubescent Boys," *Medicine and Science in Sports and Exercise* 22 (1990): 605–614; John C. Ozmun, Alan E. Mikesky, and Paul R. Surburg, "Neuromuscular Adaptations Following Prepubescent Strength Training," *Medicine and Science in Sports and Exercise* 26 (1994): 510–514; Malina, "Weight Training in Youth-Growth."

2 William J. Kraemer et al., "Resistance Training and Youth," *Pediatric Exercise Science* 1 (1989): 336–350; T. Rowland, *Children's Exercise Physiology*, 2nd ed. (Champaign, IL: Human Kinetics, 2005), 181–195.

3 Rowland, *Children's Exercise*; Ramsay et al., "Strength Training Effects in Prepubescent Boys."; C. Rians et al., "Strength Training for Prepubescent Males: Is It Safe?" *American Journal of Sports Medicine* 15 (1987): 483–489; Ozmun, Mikesky, and Surburg, "Neuromuscular Adaptations."

4 K. Häkkinen, A. Mero, and H. Kavhanen, "Specificity of Endurance, Sprint, and Strength Training on Physical Performance Capacity in Young Athletes," *Journal of Sports Medicine and Physical Fitness* 29 (1989): 27–35; B. L. Lori Thein Brody, "Endurance impairment," in *Therapeutic Exercise: Moving Toward Function*, eds. Lori Thein Brody and Carrie M. Hall (Philadelphia: Lippincott Williams & Wilkins, 1999); Scott Powers and Edward Howley, *Exercise Physiology: Theory and Application to Fitness and Performance* 4th ed. (Boston: McGraw Hill, 2001).

5 L. Matveyev, *Fundamentals of Sports Training* (Moscow: Progress, 1981); Greg Wilson et al., "The Optimal Training Load for the Development of Dynamic Athletic Performance," *Medicine and Science in Sports and Exercise* 25 no. 11 (1993): 1279–1286.

6 Xavi Schelling and Lorena Torres-Ronda, "Conditioning for Basketball: Quality and Quantity of Training," *Strength and Conditioning Journal* 35 no. 6 (Dec 2013); John Taylor, "Basketball: Applying Time Motion Data to Conditioning," *Strength and Conditioning Journal* 25 no. 2 (Apr 2003).

CHAPTER 4

Fundamental Training Principles

Periodization

Periodization involves the gradual cyclical alterations of contraction type (concentric, isometric, and eccentric, discussed in greater length later in this chapter), frequency (number of trainings per week), intensity (effort), and volume (total number of repetitions per week) in an attempt to train different muscular characteristics (hypertrophy, absolute strength, power, speed, agility).[1] In simple terms, you need to be consistently changing the workout to see muscular changes. Periodization helps the body to maximize the training effect by keeping the body in an unstable state, creating specific physical adaptations to the ever-changing demands of training. It is based on the theory that the body continually adapts to changes in the stimulus (training). Conversely, if there is no change in the training, the body will cease to make adaptations.[2] Long-term performance gains will be optimized (muscle and neural adaptation), boredom will be reduced, and the risk of overuse injuries will decrease when the exercise program is varied or changed every four to ten weeks. The variations in the workout can be as simple as changing the volume and/or intensity of the workout. It is a common mistake in the exercise and training world to see individuals not making changes in their workouts, doing the same exercises over and over again, thus limiting their opportunity to see physical changes, such as muscle growth, weight loss, and strength and endurance gains.

An important part of the periodization is active rest. There should be one to three weeks of recovery between sport seasons or training cycles to allow for physical and psychological recovery from the sport or training sessions. This is especially important for youth who play on different sports teams, specialize in one sport year-round, or participate in extracurricular conditioning activities at private training centers. During exercise training it would be appropriate to take one week off of training for every eight to twelve weeks of training.[3]

Periodization can occur over the long term or for a short time period. For example, a linear model has a training progression over a period of time, such as a year. This could mean an athlete trains for hypertrophy (muscle growth) for two months, then absolute muscle strength for two months, followed by muscular power for two months, and finally a maintenance phase where the workout volume is reduced. In the athlete, the maintenance phase is often done during the season so as to optomize sports performance.

An undulating model would have an athlete train for muscle strength, muscle endurance, and power on different days during a certain time period, perhaps twelve weeks.[4] For example, during a twelve-week training program, on Mondays, the athlete trains for muscle strength with high weight loads with three to five sets of four to eight repetitions. Muscle endurance is trained on Wednesdays, with light loads of three to five sets of fifteen repetitions using an eccentric contraction pattern (muscle lengthening contraction). On Fridays, muscle power is trained with light loads and fast muscle contractions. The bottom line is, independent of training program model, try to make consistent changes in the program design for optimal physical performance gains.

The periodization training program is broken down into two specific training cycles, macrocycle and mesocycle.

Macrocycle

The macrocycle is a long stretch of training time, possibly one year, that focuses on accomplishing a major and important fitness goal. For example, following baseball season, the athlete wants to prepare for the next season. The exercise plan for that year is the macrocycle. The macrocycle can be further broken down into mesocycles.

Mesocycle

The mesocycle is a short block of training within the macrocycle that focuses on achieving a particular goal. The mesocycle typically ranges from three to sixteen weeks and can repeat a few times within a macrocycle. The Train 2 Play mesocycles are off-season training phase (general development), off-season training phase (sport-specific power development), preseason tapering phase, and competition phase. Each of these phases would be approximately ten to fourteen weeks in length. Depending on the training needs, this ten-to-fourteen-week mesocycle can be further broken down into five-to-seven-week training blocks. In that training block, the exercises may be different, but the goals and objectives should remain the same. For example, if the athlete is in the general development phase, this phase could be broken down into two mesocycles of five weeks. The two mesocycles would have the same goal of increasing general strength in the transverse, frontal, and sagittal planes but have different training.

Train 2 Play Periodization Training Model

Off-season (general sports development phase)

The exercise portion of this phase runs for twelve weeks. The first week should be rest to recover from the previous season. The athlete may need time to heal from competition. Following the rest period, the twelve-week exercise program begins. In this phase the emphasis is on developing proper movement patterns, improving core strength and stability, and increasing base (or relative maximum) strength. If the athlete is recovering from injury, those impairments would be worked on. This is a great time to work on flexibility and musculoskeletal imbalances (muscle tightness or weakness patterns on one side of the body). The time frame would be several months before the competitive season.

For the youth and adolescent athlete, the early off-season should be a transition to another sport, which allows the athlete to recover from the previous competitive sport. For example, baseball season ends and soccer begins. The soccer season allows the shoulder and elbow to recover. The change to a different sport allows for cross training and the utilization of different muscle groups in a dramatically different way while reducing the risk of psychological burnout.

By playing multiple sports, the athlete avoids overtraining syndrome, the signs of which are decreased physical performance, general fatigue, insomnia, irritability, anxiety, loss of motivation, and lack of mental concentration. The way we do sports today, it is not uncommon for a young athlete to be overtrained, with his or her given sport being played too much. By playing multiple sports, the player is essentially developing as an all-around athlete and not a specialist. Specialization in a given sport should not occur until the growth plates are closed, which is typically in the late teenage years.

In the general development phase, the rate, duration, and pattern of work-to-recovery ratios should not mimic the competitive sport just played, allowing the body to differentiate from the competitive season.

Off-season (sport-specific development phase)

This phase runs for twelve weeks. The first week should be rest to recover from the general preparation phase. Following the week of rest, the twelve-week power conversion stage begins. In this phase, the focus is on power and anaerobic development specific to the sport. There is a movement from general exercise to specific development of muscle groups that are utilized in the sport. In this phase, the goal is to gain maximum strength, power, force, agility, speed, and quickness while meeting the demands of the sport. The athlete should see increased muscle growth (hypertrophy of fast-twitch muscle fibers for power and hypertrophy of slow-twitch muscle fibers for endurance). We are creating a better sport-specific athlete through sport-specific fitness and training. For example, a basketball player would go through explosive exercises such as medicine ball throws, sprints, and plyometric jumping.

Preseason (tapering phase)

This phase starts with one week off of training. This twelve-week block involves a large reduction in training load and stress with an emphasis on sports performance and skill development. The individual skill of the sport becomes the primary exercises used in training. The body is becoming optimally prepared for the upcoming competition or season. The goal is to improve the rate of energy production and power needed for the sport. The energy production needs to be specific to the sport being played. For example, a soccer player should be doing agility, speed, and quickness drills that replicate the demands of the sport.

During the preseason, it is common to see many sports-related injuries. Often, this is due to the volume, intensity, and frequency of exercise. "Too much, too fast, too soon." In high-speed running sports (basketball, soccer, lacrosse, field hockey, and so on) it is essential to give at least one to two days' rest between high-speed training activities. For example, the football coach is ambitious in preparing his team for the season. Assuming each player did not have a specific preparation training phase, the coach runs the players two times a day. This volume, intensity, and frequency of running can be too much. This leads to microtrauma, breakdown, and injury. Overuse injuries of the lower extremities are commonplace in this type of scenario, such as stress fractures (foot), Achilles tendinosis (ankle), patellofemoral syndrome (knee), and hip bursitis (hip).

Exercise and conditioning for team sports in the preseason faces the dilemma of how best to combine speed, agility, and endurance while incorporating tactical and skill work. The work-to-rest ratio is critical to keep in mind while training for the season. Work-to-rest ratios could fall anywhere between one to one or one to six work to rest depending on the condition of the athlete entering the preseason and the demands of the sport. For example, a work-to-rest ratio of one to six would mean that if it took thirty seconds to perform a high-speed agility drill, the athlete would rest for one hundred eighty seconds (three minutes) before performing the next drill. The work-to-rest ratio is dependent on the intensity of the exercise. The more intense the speed, agility, or plyometric exercise, the greater the work-to-rest ratio. In order to have speed, agility, and power gains, the muscles must be trained at or near the 100 percent intensity effort level. If the exercise intensity is not maintained at that high level, the muscle training becomes more for endurance versus power and explosiveness. The ultimate goal is to peak for the season. Training volume, intensity, and frequency should be tapered at the appropriate time to allow an elevated preparedness for the pending season.

Tapering should begin eight to fourteen days prior to the game or competition. The first part is to reduce the training frequency to about 80 percent of the pre-taper training phase. The volume of training should be reduced to 40–60 percent of the pre-taper training phase. The intensity is maintained at moderate-high ratio to avoid a detraining effect.[5]

Competition phase

This phase runs for approximately twelve weeks or the length of the season. The athlete is now competing in his or her sport. If time permits, this is a great time to enter a maintenance program to sufficiently maintain strength and power gains. It has been determined that a once-weekly maintenance program was as sufficient as a twice-weekly maintenance program in retaining strength gains made after twelve weeks of resistance training in adolescent athletes.[6]

In a research study, it was observed that children who participated in a ten-week plyometric training program prior to the start of the soccer season were able to maintain training-induced gains in power after eight weeks of reduced training, which included soccer practice.[7]

When competition begins, one of the most challenging aspects of training is to continue to optimize the physiological gains obtained during the season. Furthermore, while continuing the training during the season, it is imperative to not produce excessive fatigue and stress that hampers sports performance.

If the athlete is playing multiple sports as advised, the competitive phase of one sport could be the specific sports development phase of another sport. For example, during basketball season the athlete could be in the specific sports phase for baseball. In this scenario, the athlete would work on linear and rotational ballistic patterns to enhance throwing and hitting power for baseball season. The muscle groups used in these exercises would be different than those used in basketball. However, you would have to closely monitor the athlete to assure the exercise program is not negatively affecting the competitive phase of basketball.

For those adolescent or adult athletes who have now specialized in a sport, the above-mentioned training phases are ideal for optimal physiological gains to enhance sports performance. For the child, the emphasis is on inspiring them to be active in exercise and sport. Aggressively sticking to the above-mentioned phases and timelines may be too rigorous for the younger athlete. This is where the parent, coach, or trainer may need to adapt the training to meet the needs of the child.

The Train 2 Play philosophy is that exercise and conditioning is a lifelong activity to be continued long after competitive sports are completed in order to maintain optimal health and quality of life.

Set Goals and Training Objectives

Prior to starting an exercise program, the trainer, coach, parent, and/or athlete should create reasonable goals and objectives. This should be done with the athlete so that he or she feels part of the training process. In defining a goal, it is the destination to be achieved—for example, to become a starting pitcher on the middle school baseball team next season. The goal should be specific, measurable, achievable, relevant, and time-based.[8] Objectives are the milestones you need to reach in order to achieve that goal, such as increase pitch velocity by five miles per hour by improving medicine ball rotational throw with good sequencing, control, and velocity. Objectives are smaller benchmarks that are based and derived from the main goal. As the athlete reaches the objectives, he or she is on the way to reaching the ultimate goal. The goal should be fun, believable, and attainable through hard work. The goal can be a great motivator in training and in life.

Youth and Adolescent Resistance Safety Considerations and Guidelines

It is imperative that the youth and adolescent exercise training program be safe, effective, and enjoyable. The trainer must have an appreciation of the physical and psychosocial uniqueness of the athlete being trained. There is no minimum age requirement for an exercise program; however, the young athlete must be mentally and physically ready to comply with instructions and undergo the physical stress and demands of a training program. In general, if the child is participating in sport activities and general age-appropriate play (generally age six to eight years), he or she should be able to perform some type of training that is specific to the individual. In chapter 2 we reviewed the research on safety and effectiveness of exercise for youth and adolescent athletes.

In designing any personalized exercise training program, one must consider the medical history, age, level of physical maturity, sport-specific skill level, preferred sport, training experience, and present fitness level of the athlete. We recommend a medical examination before participation in our Train 2 Play exercise training program. In most cases there should be no issues; however, medical clearance is an important first step prior to beginning any exercise training program. At the youth and adolescent level, instruction and supervision must be provided by adults who have a general understanding of exercise training needs, goals, and the participant's interest and motivation levels. The exercise program should be enjoyable and fun to all participants. This is an opportunity for coaches, trainers, and parents to teach youth about healthy lifestyle choices such as proper nutrition, adequate sleep, stress management, and regular physical activity.[9]

In our Train 2 Play exercise programs we emphasize basic movement patterns, proper lifting techniques, safety procedures, and specific methods of progression. Finally, children and adolescents must not be treated as miniature adults, nor should adult exercise guidelines and training philosophies be imposed on youth.

Exercise Experience

Prior to beginning training, it is important to determine the athlete's exercise experience. It is essential to select exercises that are appropriate for the individual's body size, fitness level, and exercise experience. Regardless of the athlete's experience level, basic movement patterns must be perfected to develop a base of motor control and strength. It is important to gradually progress to more advanced multi-joint movements as confidence and competence develops. To obtain maximum gains in fitness and reduce the risk of injury, it is essential to first learn how to move well and perform each exercise correctly with no load or a light load and then gradually progress the training intensity, volume, and load without compromising exercise technique.

In the Train 2 Play method, athletes can be divided into three categories: novice, experienced, and advanced. For our purposes, novice refers to an individual who has no or limited exercise training experience (less than two to three months) or an individual who has not trained for several months. The novice athlete would work out one to two times per week for around thirty minutes each. The experienced athlete could work out two to three times per week for thirty to forty-five minutes each. The advanced athlete refers to an individual with at least twelve months of training experience who has also attained significant improvements in muscular strength, power, agility, and speed. Our advanced athlete could work out up to three times per week for forty-five to sixty minutes. The more advanced the athlete, the greater progression to functional sports-specific training. Based on age, we can further divide guidelines for the exercise routine.

Ages 6–8: One to two workouts per week for about twenty to thirty minutes each, with a focus on basic movement patterns and beginner exercises. Keep it as fun as possible, inspiring the child to enjoy exercise and movement. The ABCs (agility, balance, coordination, and strength) of physical development are essential baseline components of the beginning athlete. These ABCs set the foundation for future athletic development.

Ages 9–11: Two to three workouts per week for about thirty minutes each, mastering basic movement patterns and beginning multiple joint movement patterns with low load. The ABCs should be further enhanced and developed. There can be focus on the beginnings of a plyometric exercise routine that would help in the development of power and explosiveness.

Ages 11–12: Two to three workouts per week for about thirty to forty-five minutes each. Basic movement patterns should be mastered and multiple joint movement patterns should be utilized for whole body functional training. There is a progression of the emphasis on developing power, explosiveness, speed, and agility. The athlete could follow a year-round periodization training program (described above) which would include a general off-season exercise training program, specific off-season exercise training program, preseason exercise training program, and in-season exercise training program.

Ages 13–15: Two to three workouts per week for about forty-five to sixty minutes each. This young athlete is reaching puberty and peak height velocity (discussed in detail in chapter 7) where hormones are being released, enhancing his or her development. In males, testosterone and growth hormone allow the athlete to gain muscle mass and size. The emphasis moves to resistive training in a sport-specific manner based on muscle groups and movement patterns utilized for the sport. This is an ideal opportunity to improve power, explosiveness, speed, and agility. The athlete should seriously follow a year-round periodization training program to take advantage of the body's natural abilities for growth and physical development.

Ages 16 and beyond: Three to five workouts per week for about forty-five to ninety minutes each. This developed athlete has reached puberty (and thus has reached or will soon reach peak height velocity) where hormones like testosterone and growth hormone have allowed for optimal development of the neuromuscular system. The emphasis is to train in a sport-specific manner based on muscle groups and movement patterns utilized for the sport. At this time, the athlete will have the opportunity to express and gain his or her maximum strength, power, explosiveness, speed, and agility. In order to optimize athleticism, it is vital that the athlete follow a year-round periodization training program at this phase of his or her athletic career.

Exercise Grading System

Progression of exercise can be difficult for even the experienced physical therapist or trainer. However, the appropriate progression of training is essential to optimize physiological gains and to prevent injury. In the Train 2 Play method, we use a grading scale with every exercise to determine appropriate exercise progression. Every exercise is a test and should be consistently evaluated for form and function. The exercises should be challenging (a task that tests abilities) but not too difficult (a movement that is hard to accomplish or understand). For ease and simplicity, the scale goes from 0 to 2, with 0 being unable to perform the exercise or it is painful and 2 being the individual has mastered the movement pattern or exercise.

Train 2 Play Sports Grading Scale for the Progression of Exercise

Grading Scale	Description	Action
0	Unable to perform exercise or it is painful	Simplify the exercise by going slower and/or breaking down its components into simpler movements. If this does not help, regress back to the previous exercise. If it is a new exercise, consider waiting and adding the exercise at a later date.
1	Form is adequate with some mistakes and compensations during the movement	Stay with this exercise. Consider slowing down the motion or lessening a component of the complexity.
2	Perfect or near-perfect form in movement with relative ease	Progress athlete by adding or increasing weight, adding isometric or eccentric muscle contractions, moving from a stable to an unstable surface, or adding a multiple joint movement exercise.

Train 2 Play Training Terminology and Principles

The following definitions are commonly used in Train 2 Play writings and are some of the aspects we place great focus on when creating individualized training models. A knowledge of these terms and ideas will help parents, coaches, trainers, and athletes create a well-balanced training program that works out the entire body in several different ways.

Specific Adaptation to Imposed Demand (SAID) Principle

The specificity of training is essential to optimizing sports performance and preventing injury. One of the most important physical therapy training theories is the SAID principle, which stands for specific adaptation to imposed demand. The SAID principle states that if the body is put under a specific stress (physical or mental) of varying intensity and duration, the body will attempt to overcome that stress by adapting specifically to the demand of the stress.[10] The basic tenant of the SAID principle is that the body will adapt specifically to the training at hand. For example, if an athlete wants to hit a baseball far or throw a baseball hard, the athlete must train to replicate the specific movements and muscle contraction types of the swing and throwing motion. In the baseball example, medicine ball exercises are a great way to create specific movements that will lead to sport-specific adaptations in the throw or swing. The training must have an intensity and resistance that loads the body beyond its capabilities in order to have the physical adaptations that lead to increases in strength, speed, endurance, and resilience to recovery.

One-Repetition Maximum Test (1RM)

The one-repetition maximum test is the gold standard in assessing the strength capacity of an individual. It is the maximum amount of weight an individual can lift for one repetition with correct mechanical form. The 1RM is the starting point to determine the weight to be utilized during the training. The 1RM has been shown to be safe and reliable for youth and adolescent athletes.

This is the basic 1RM test procedure:

1. Perform a dynamic stretch warm-up.
2. Perform a warm-up set of a selected load with approximately 50 percent of predicted 1RM for six to ten repetitions. For example, perform six back squats at 50 percent predicted weight.
3. Rest for one to five minutes.
4. Perform a second set of the exercise at 80 percent of the predicted 1RM for three repetitions. For example, perform three back squats at 80 percent predicted weight.
5. Rest for one to five minutes.
6. Increase the load by 5–10 percent for upper body and 10–20 percent for lower body for one repetition. Continue increasing load until the 1RM is achieved. For example, perform one back squat then increase the weight by 10 percent. Rest and repeat again until maximum weight is reached. Rest period should remain one to five minutes for each repetition.

Drill or Exercise Selection

The selection of exercises should be goal and sports specific and involve multiple muscles and joint movements. This can vary depending on the volume, load, recovery, intensity, and drill complexity. In order to be complete in body development, our training program involves exercises performed with a variety of contraction types—concentric, isometric, and eccentric—using all planes of available motion—horizontal row, horizontal press, vertical pull, vertical press, legs (posterior, anterior, and chain), and core (frontal, transverse, and sagittal planes). Once the athlete develops adequate strength in the above-mentioned planes, plyometrics, speed, and agility (change of direction) training can be added.

Triplanar Movement Patterns

Being a great athlete starts with the ability to finely move your body explosively through three planes of motion. In order to move your body through these planes of motion, it is essential to have optimal strength, endurance, flexibility, and coordination. A lack of ability to move in these planes will often lead to energy leaks in the system. An energy leak is when the body expends more energy and time to complete the movement than needed, thus leading to diminished performance.

Since most sports-related movements involve the use of all three planes of motion, exercises that are triplanar are said to be more functional and sports-specific. There are three primary planes of movement of the body: sagittal, frontal, and transverse.

1. **Sagittal Plane Strength Training:** Sagittal plane movements occur from front to back. Examples of these would be a horizontal row, horizontal press, squat, lunge, or core plank.

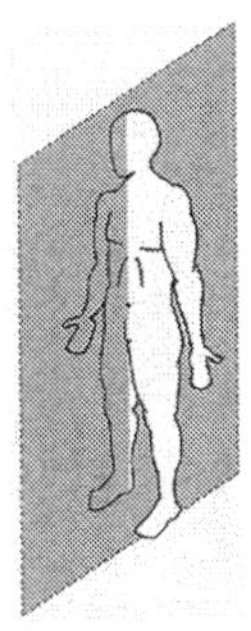

2. **Frontal Plane Strength Training:** Frontal plane movements occur from side to side. Examples of these would be a vertical pull, vertical press, lateral leg movement, or core side plank.

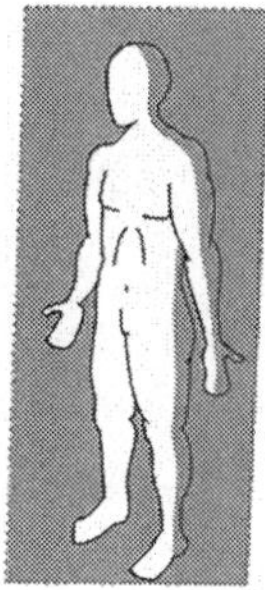

3. **Transverse Plane Strength Training:** Transverse plane movements occur in a circular fashion around the body. An example would be core rotational exercise such as a medicine ball toss from the side.[11]

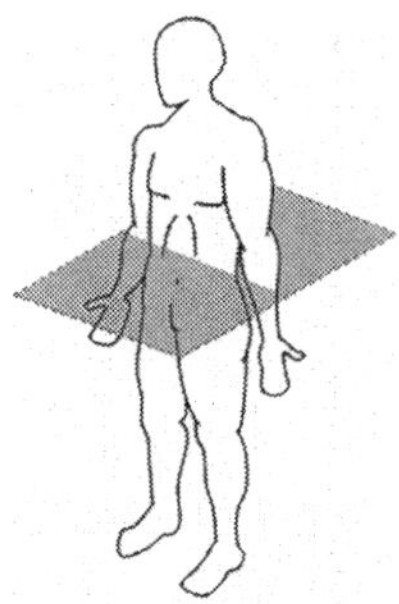

Multiplanar Strength Training

Multiplanar movement is any movement that occurs through a combination of the planes of motion. Complex movement patterns are often done in plyometrics, jumping, and speed/agility. For example, any sport involving hitting or throwing starts with a frontal plane movement with the transfer of body weight from back to front. Once the weight is transferred to the front side of the body, rotation begins, which occurs in the transverse plane. Many sports are like this, such as golf, lacrosse, tennis, field hockey, ice hockey, cricket, softball, and baseball. All of the swing sports first have a transfer of weight from back to front in the frontal plane and then a rotational component in the transverse plane. Now if your training only involves exercise in the sagittal or frontal plane, the training is missing a key component in sports-specific training. This lack of complete training can lead to energy leaks or weakness in the body that will negatively impact the athlete's performance. This could be noticed as reduced swing velocity due to inadaquate training of the rotational component in the transverse plane.

The body has the unique ability to couple movements in sequenced patterns. When the movement pattern is sequenced in a timely manner with efficiency, the energy is stacked and transferred up the kinetic chain, which is a connection of body segments (e.g., foot, ankle, leg, knee). The energy passes from the ground reaction forces through the legs to the hips, torso, and then arms for a ballistic explosion upon the object. Another way to think of the transfer of energy up the kinetic chain is the "cracking" of a whip. A person holding the whip rapidly moves their arm in a downward fashion. The energy from the individual is passed down to the whip, eventually reaching its end. The energy that is imparted is added or stacked, leading to a large release of energy heard as a load "crack." Like "cracking" a whip, using multiplanar movements causes the stacking of energy through the body, increasing force output.

Sequencing of Drills or Exercises

The sequencing of drills or exercises should start with a dynamic warm-up. This is a way to ramp up the body, preparing it for higher-level function training. There is a training hierarchy that should be followed during the workout:[12]

- highest power output exercises before lower power exercises
- larger muscle groups before smaller
- multiple-joint movements before single-joint exercises
- higher-intensity before lower-intensity exercises

This is a simple way to progress the exercises to get the most out of every training session.

Progressive Overload

Progressive overload is the gradual increase of stress placed upon the body during exercise training. The Train 2 Play method emphasizes the use of the principle of overload in a safe and progressive manner. Overload causes the neuromuscular systems to adapt to the changing load or stressor. For the neuromuscular system to adapt maximally to the training load (stress), the type of muscle contraction, volume, and intensity must be altered frequently. If there is no overload, then the concomitant adaptive changes will eventually stop, lessening the effectiveness of the exercise program. Progressive overload is accomplished by altering training variables such as contraction type, intensity, repetitions, resistance, speed/tempo, or rest periods.[13] Without progressive overload, there will be minimal changes in muscular growth, development, and performance.

According to the American College of Sports Medicine, it is recommended that a 2–10 percent increase in load be applied when the individual can perform the current workload for one to two repetitions over the desired number.[14] For example, an athlete is able to perform a squat exercise for three sets of ten repetitions at two hundred pounds. A progression would be to increase the weight by 10 percent to 220 pounds. In this case, the athlete could reduce the repetitions to eight for three sets. Also, training using a variety of muscle contraction types (concentric, isometric, and eccentric) can add to the training effect.

Muscle Hypertrophy

Muscle hypertrophy occurs when there is an increase in size of the cellular components of skeletal muscle. The increase in muscle cell size increases the overall size of the muscle while increasing overall strength. In order to get optimal muscle hypertrophy, three to five sets with six to twelve repetitions using one to two minute rest periods between sets should be used. A training speed of moderate velocity is recommended.[15]

Muscular Strength

Strength refers to maximal force that specific muscles or muscle groups can generate at a specified velocity. Strength occurs over three different types of muscle contractions—concentric, eccentric, and isometric. Concentric and eccentric muscle contractions are also known as isotonic contractions. All movements of the human body involve these three types of muscle contractions. With that, in order to optimize muscular development for sports performance, it is essential to train utilizing each muscle contraction type. In order to optimize strength, a muscle should be trained concentrically, eccentrically, and isometrically in the sagittal, frontal, and transverse planes. The Train 2 Play method uses triphasic muscle contraction types through multiplanar movement patterns. This approach uses the entire muscle contraction spectrum with all available movement planes. This approach should provide the best training opportunity to improve physical development and performance.

In order to optimize strength, lighter loads of 0–60 percent of the one-repetition maximum for lower body exercises and 30–60 percent of the one-repetition maximum for upper body exercises should be used. The contraction velocity should be moderately fast with three to five minutes of rest between sets. Three to five sets of six to twelve repetitions is recommended.[16]

In order to optimize performance and athleticism, all athletes need to optimize their relative maximum strength (strength relative to one's body weight). The more strength an athlete has, the more they are able to build power, agility, quickness, and speed. Getting stronger is a crucial component of building a solid foundation of athletics.

Muscular Endurance

To obtain muscular endurance, it is recommended that light to moderate loads of 40–60 percent of the one-repetition maximum be performed at higher repetitions of fifteen or more using less than ninety-second rest periods between sets.[17]

Muscular Power

The ability to generate power is one of the most important factors that separates good athletes from great athletes. In a research article in *Sports Health*, it was determined that the single best predictor of elite-level athletic status was that individual's ability to create maximal power.[18]

What makes up power? From a physics perspective, an athlete uses his strength to produce a force on himself or an object, such as a bat, ball, ground, or person, causing movement. The movement is defined as work (force × distance). If that work occurs very rapidly over a brief period of time, it is then called power (force × distance/time). Simply put, when you put speed and strength together, you get power. For example, a baseball player hitting a home run or a basketball player exploding to the basket to dunk a ball demonstrates power. The best way to create power in an athlete is plyometric exercise training. To increase power, the athlete must either increase the load of the object to be moved (force) or increase the velocity (decrease the time) at which the object or himself is moved. For example, in the ten-pound medicine ball throwing exercises, the ball is thrown as fast as possible against a wall. The ten-pound medicine ball represents the resistance or load to be moved. This requires strength to move the medicine ball. The act of throwing it hard represents the velocity. Thus, medicine ball throws can be an example of an exercise to develop power.

When attempting to develop power, it is important to address two fundamental questions:

1. Does the athlete have sufficient base strength or relative maximum strength to produce or build the required power? For example, if the individual has poor core strength in the side plank position, it would not be appropriate to perform medicine ball plyometric rotational tosses due to a poor base of relative strength. In this case the athlete may have poor mechanics, leading to a poor training effect or even injury. Once the base core strength is developed, the individual can then produce sufficient power to perform plyometric rotational exercises.
2. Does the athlete have the motor control ability to perform basic movement patterns as a precursor to the power performance moves? For example, if the individual does not have the ability to squat properly, adding resistance to develop power would not be recommended. First, the individual should be able to move with good form and efficiency then progress to resistance. Power development will happen best when the athlete first has strong

efficient fundamental movement patterns, then power training can begin.

Isometric Muscle Contraction

Isometric muscle contraction is a type of muscle contraction in which the joint angle and muscle length do not change. During the isometric contraction there is increased muscle contraction force due to greater motor unit (series of muscle cells) recruitment and a higher muscle firing rate. The increased muscle tension creates the opportunity for muscle hypertrophy and strengthening in that given range of motion. An example of an isometric contraction would be an abdominal plank exercise in which the athlete holds the plank position for a period of time.

Isometric training can be performed in two ways. First, a movement can be performed and held at mid or end range. For example, perform a single leg squat and lower to approximately 120 degrees of knee bend. Hold that position for five seconds. Explode concentrically out of this position to the start position. Second, perform a dynamic movement and hold or stick the landing or position. For example, perform a lateral jump, then stick and hold the landing for five seconds. Explode concentrically out of this position to the start position. In this case you coach the athlete to hit the ground like a brick, hold for five seconds, and explode back to the starting point.

Concentric Muscle Contraction

Concentric muscle contraction is a type of muscle contraction in which the joint angle decreases and muscle length shortens. Most exercise training programs use just the concentric muscle contraction type. An example would be a biceps curl exercise in which the elbow bends and the biceps muscle shortens during a contraction. The biceps contracts concentrically to bend the elbow, bringing the hand close to the shoulder. A concentric exercise recruits more of the muscle at the same resistance. More energy is used for concentric work as compared to eccentric work, which is why individuals can't exercise as long when doing concentric exercise. As velocity increases, concentric force capacity decreases. Concentric muscle contraction creates the least force of the three muscle contraction types (eccentric creates the most force, followed by isometric). However, during plyometric movements, during the concentric phase, the greatest power is produced. This is due to the stacking of forces from the stretch reflex and stretch-shortening cycle (described later in the text).

Eccentric Muscle Contraction

Eccentric muscle contraction is a type of muscle contraction in which the joint angle increases and the muscle is lengthened while under load. Eccentric training focuses on slowing down the elongation of the muscle in order to challenge the muscles, which can lead to increased muscular strength, improved muscle healing and repair, and increased metabolic rate.[19]

Eccentric muscle action generates 10–40 percent more force than concentric contractions with less work. It is an essential contraction type for the rehabilitation of muscle tendon overuse injuries, injury prevention, and sports performance training. Eccentric training extends the time under tension, allowing neurological adaptation activity through the muscle spindle and Golgi tendon organ. These small nerve cells in the muscle increase the contraction force when stimulated. Also, this preferentially recruits type II, high threshold, fast-twitch muscle, which is essential for explosive power. Delayed-onset muscle soreness (DOMS) increases with eccentric muscle contractions.

The Train 2 Play training method employs two types of eccentric training: slow eccentric pattern and eccentric-concentric pattern, also called shock pattern. The slow eccentric pattern movement is done slowly for a count of five seconds followed by a rapid concentric contraction. For example, in the push-up exercise, the body is slowly lowered down to a count of five seconds. When the athlete reaches the bottom of the movement, they rapidly contract, pushing up to the starting position. The eccentric-concentric pattern is described below in the plyometric training section.

Eccentric muscle training has been shown to improve strength and power by up to 3.5 times as compared to concentric training alone.[20] Eccentric training alone has been shown to increase vertical jump height by 8–11 percent.[21]

The American College of Sports Medicine's position statement on concentric, eccentric, and isometric exercise is "The optimal characteristics of strength-specific programs include the use of concentric, eccentric, and isometric muscle actions and the performance of bilateral and unilateral single- and multiple-joint exercises."[22]

Plyometric Training

Plyometric training is a specialized exercise training method that consists of dynamic and rapid stretching of muscles (eccentric action) immediately followed by a shortening muscle contraction (concentric action) of the same muscles and tissues. This type of exercise training is designed to produce speed, strength, and ballistic power to enhance sports performance. The plyometric stretch-shortening cycle has three phases, which are described below.

1. **Eccentric phase (pre-stretch or negative):** The eccentric phase (muscle lengthening contraction) has also been described as the readiness, preloading, presetting, preparatory, or countermovement phase. This phase stretches tiny nerve endings in the muscle that enhances the subsequent muscle contractions. As the muscle is lengthened, the noncontractile parts of the muscle are stretched, creating a rubber band or spring effect. When the muscle contracts and shortens, the noncontractile parts of the muscle "snap back," adding energy and force to the contraction. These two components lead to increased muscle function and performance from a neurological and biomechanical perspective. This eccentric pre-stretch will enhance the resultant concentric muscle contraction.[23]

   During the eccentric pre-stretch phase, there are three factors that can influence or enhance the training: magnitude of the stretch, rate of the stretch, and duration of the stretch. Manipulating any of these variables will have a significant effect on the amount of energy stored during the eccentric pre-stretch motion.

2. **Isometric phase (amortization phase):** The amortization phase is the time delay from the end of the eccentric phase to the onset of the concentric phase. In this phase there is an isometric

contraction, or stabilization of the joint, prior to the concentric contraction. For the eccentric-concentric pattern, the movement is performed in a rapid, ballistic manner. The muscles are loaded and unloaded quickly.

The isometric contraction is essential in movement as it provides an energy transfer station for all muscle actions, turning absorbed eccentric energy into dynamic or explosive concentric muscle actions. The shorter the amortization phase, the more effective and powerful the plyometric movement. The quick movement from eccentric to concentric contraction allows the stored energy to be stacked, or added, to the movement. During the eccentric muscle contraction, energy is absorbed and stored by the musculotendinous unit (the muscle and tendon combined). According to the law of conservation of energy, the greater the velocity of the stretch during the eccentric contraction, the greater the amount of potential or stored elastic energy that can be recovered and contributed to the concentric muscle contraction. The shorter the time elapsed the greater the spring or rubber band effect. If the stretch-shortening cycle is slow, the muscles lose elastic energy. If the amortization phase is delayed or slowed, the stored energy is wasted as heat and the stretch reflex is not activated, leading to less force development during the concentric contraction phase. The time between eccentric and concentric contraction (the amortization phase) should be as rapid as possible, less than .15 seconds. This rubber band effect can add up to 180 percent contraction force to the movement as compared to maximal isometric or concentric muscle contraction.[24]

A strong isometric muscle contraction during dynamic movement acts like a block, or strong base, for the muscles to contract against. Without this strong isometric contraction, there is less power development for the next muscle contraction and movement. This is known as an energy or power leak. For example, during throwing and hitting sports, energy moves up the kinetic chain starting with the ground reaction forces at push-off. The energy moves to the stiff front side (caused by isometric contraction of the thigh muscles). This strong front-side contraction provides the stable base, allowing the hips to rotate. The hips then become the stable base (isometric contraction), allowing the trunk and torso to rotate. Lastly, the trunk and torso become the stable base (isometric contraction) for the scapula and arms to move. If there is lack of isometric contraction stabilizing each of these body segments, the movement is weakened and energy is leaked.

A second example is an elite basketball player who makes a quick lateral change of direction. The athlete must perform a strong eccentric contraction followed by a brief isometric contraction (.1 second) great enough to completely stop his or her directional energy before concentrically contracting, reaccelerating in a different direction. If the athlete has weakness in that isometric contraction to temporarily stop the movement, this could represent a "weak link" in the movement pattern. Remember that the athlete is only as strong as his or her weakest link. Inadequate performance during isometric contraction results in less force available for absorption and a subsequent decrease in force output. Poor isometric strength during movement leads to a slower and decreased rate of energy absorption, which leads to less power to be transferred during the stretch-shortening cycle and concentric movement. A great athlete diverts maximum energy from eccentric directly to concentric with little loss of energy. Without training, most athletes have energy leaks which impede movement, reduce sports performance, and increase potential for injury.

3. **Concentric phase:** The concentric phase is a muscle-shortening contraction. This final phase is the culmination of the previous events of the elastic properties of the prestretched muscles and the neurological stretch reflex. The body's neurologic system has a way of protecting the muscle from being stretched or contracted excessively. This protective system can actually be trained to enhance the muscle contraction. The Golgi tendon organ (GTO) is a protective mechanism that senses the amount of tension in a contracting muscle. If the tension in the muscle increases beyond safe limits, the GTO fires, limiting or shutting down the muscle contraction. Eccentric training can desensitize the GTO, allowing the athlete to absorb higher levels of force without triggering an inhibitory GTO reflex. The muscle spindle is a nerve ending

found in the muscle that detects static or dynamic stretch of the muscle. It is designed to protect the contracting muscle from being stretched beyond the muscle's limits. When the muscle is stretched like in an eccentric muscle contraction, a strong nerve impulse is sent to the spinal cord. This triggers a strong nerve impulse back to the muscle, enhancing the concentric muscle contraction and limiting the amount of stretch. Proper training can enhance muscle spindle activity, stimulating a stronger, more powerful concentric muscle contraction that can improve sports performance. Regardless of the exercise, the concentric phase of contraction should be done at maximum intensity of effort. Instruct the athlete to "explode" or "fire" into the movement.[25]

In a meta-analysis of plyometric training exercises, it was determined that greatest improvements occurred with a training volume of less than ten weeks and a minimum of fifteen sessions. During the sessions, the training should build to high-intensity effort with a maximum of eighty combined jumps per session for trained athletes.[26]

Force-Velocity Curve

The description of the force-velocity relationship in muscles was first described by English exercise science researcher Archibald Hill in 1938. The force generated by a muscle depends on the total number of fibers attached and contracting. The amount of muscle fibers contracting is affected by time. The greater the time of contraction the more muscle fibers contracting. There is an inverse relationship between force and velocity. Simply put, when a muscle increases force, there is a decrease in velocity and vice versa. Higher force muscle contractions produce greater strength. For example, as you can see in the graph below, powerlifting is often associated with lifting heavy weights. The heavier the weight lifted the greater number of muscle fibers contracting. The greater number of muscle fibers contracting leads to less velocity in the movement. In the middle of the graph, you see medicine ball throws. This is utilized in our baseball training program. The medicine ball is lighter in weight and can be thrown at a moderate velocity with fewer muscle fibers contracting. At the end of the spectrum is the sprint. A sprint is done with no weight (resistance), therefore it can be performed at maximum velocity and minimal force. For our purposes, the force-velocity curve illustrates the importance of training the muscle in a periodized manner through a wide variety of resistances, contraction types, and speeds in order to optimize the training effect.

Force-Velocity Curve

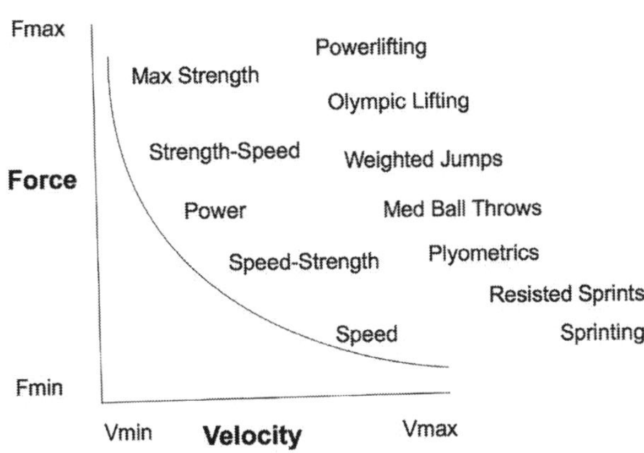

Complex Training/Post-Activation Potentiation Training (PAP)

PAP is an exercise training theory in which the contractile history of a muscle influences the mechanical performance of subsequent muscle contractions. PAP training increases muscle force and rate of force development as a result of previous activation of the muscle.[27] It typically involves the combination of a potentially heavy, loaded exercise followed by a biomechanically similar plyometric activity that is sports specific. For example, a squat exercise is followed by plyometric box jumps.

The current research, conducted on competitive athletes from three different sport disciplines, confirmed the effectiveness of PAP of the upper and lower limbs, thus improving performance in explosive, sport-specific movements.[28]

As part of the Train 2 Play specific off-season training program, the first set of the exercise the athlete performs would be an eccentric contraction followed by an isometric hold contraction of five seconds before going into the concentric movement. The athlete would then perform the same exercise on the other side. Immediately following this exercise, the athlete would perform the second set in a plyometric or ballistic fashion. For example, with the lateral lunge to rotational medicine ball toss exercise, the athlete's first set includes the lateral lunge in which the athlete bends the knee and lowers (eccentric contraction). The athlete holds that position for five seconds (isometric contraction). The athlete then raises to the starting position (concentric contraction). The second set of the exercise is done in a plyometric fashion. The medicine ball is thrown to the athlete who quickly loads and explosively throws the medicine ball back to the person or against the wall. Because of the intensity of the muscle contraction, four to eight repetitions should be used with two to four minutes of rest between sets.

Progression for Learning New Movement Patterns

Exercise progression can be difficult for even the most astute training professional. When first performing a novel task or movement, the brain and motor system is not in sync, and the movement is often of poor quality. When an athlete repeats a specific movement over and over again, the brain records these movement patterns in what's called an engram. The more these movement patterns are done the more they become second nature. No thought is needed to perform the movement. The brain then can use these movement patterns during competition. If the movement pattern is faulty, this could lead to poor movement, aberrant function, poor sports performance, and injury. The poor movement is inefficient, causing an energy leak.

Independent of the new movement pattern to be learned, there is a certain progression by the brain and motor system that is essential to create optimal learning of the engram. If the brain learns an incorrect movement, that faulty movement will be repeated during function and performance. In order to perfect the movement, it is essential to follow the below steps when learning a new movement pattern. Each step is followed by an example.

1. Start slow and move to fast movements. Perform a lunge slow, concentrating and thinking about proper movement and alignment before performing quick lunges.
2. Break down the task to its simple components and then progress to more complex movements. Perform a modified push-up (on knees instead of on toes) before performing a standard push-up (on toes).
3. Progress from low-level to high-level movement activities. Perform a double leg squat with proper form and alignment before progressing to a single leg squat with arm raises.
4. Progress from stable to unstable movements. Perform a standing squat and then progress to a squat on a BOSU ball.
5. Progress from active to reactive movements. Catch a ball while stationary before progressing to catching a ball while moving laterally.
6. Progress from predictable to unpredictable movements. Move from catching a ball while moving laterally to catching a ball that is thrown in any direction.

When learning a new movement or novel task, the athlete should:

- hear it
- see it
- feel it
- repeat it
- perfect it

Instability Resistance Training

Instability resistance training (IRT) involves resistance exercises performed on an unstable surface or device. IRT devices are very popular in current training facilities. These instability devices include Swiss balls/gym balls, BOSU balls, foam rollers, wobble boards, suspended chains, ropes, and other devices. The advantage of IRT is that it provides optimal balance and coordination training, which promotes neural adaptation, but it does forfeit strength and power development.

Studies that investigate force or power output during exercises on unstable surfaces conclude that there is up to a 29 percent decrease in power and force. For example, if an athlete was to do a squat on a BOSU ball or flat ground, he or she would be able to do more weight on flat ground, thereby increasing strength. However, if the goal is to improve balance and proprioception (joint position sense), IRT has been shown to improve balance by 105 percent as opposed to stable-base exercises. When looking at IRT from a functional performance perspective, IRT provides increases in strength, power, and speed up to 30 percent in functional or complex movements such as agility runs, sprinting, and balance and coordination activities, all of which require high levels of core stability.[29]

The inability to stabilize and balance our bodies leads to leaks in energy, reducing power and force output. For example, lower-extremity balance deficiencies have been linked to shoulder dysfunction. A research study showed that a throwing athlete who had greater shoulder dysfunction also had greater deficits in lower extremity balance and stability.[30] In order to throw a baseball, functional stability, muscular strength, and endurance are required around the core, particularly the hips, lumbar spine, and scapula (shoulder blade). The core musculature becomes active in a feed-forward fashion during upper-extremity movement. In sports or activities that require a great degree of limb movement, the core provides a foundation for the muscles of the arms and legs to move against. In this case, the baseball player could perform shoulder exercises while standing on a half foam roller. The athlete would be increasing strength of the shoulder while improving balance and stability of the core.[31]

Supersetting

Supersetting involves training opposing muscle groups—agonists and antagonists—with minimal rest between exercises. For example, a bicep curl followed by a tricep extension would be a superset. The Train 2 Play method employs supersetting with some of the exercise programs.

Compound Setting

Compound setting is performing two different exercises of the same muscle group in alternating fashion with little to no rest between exercises. An example is performing a squat exercise followed by box jumps. In this case, we are using similar muscle groups in both the squat and the jump; however, they are different exercises. The Train 2 Play method employs compound setting with some of the exercise programs.

Alternating Exercise Setting

Alternating exercise setting is when two exercises are performed right after each other involving different body parts and muscle groups. For example, an upper body push followed by a lower body pull exercise. Collectively, these methods allow more exercises to be completed within a session and allow greater intensity of each exercise due to extended recovery of each muscle group being worked. The Train 2 Play method employs alternating exercise setting with some of the exercise programs.

High-Intensity Interval Training (HIIT)

Scientific evidence shows that the number of repetitions, the resistance, and the rest between sets are important factors to the development of metabolic stress. Remember, metabolic stress is essential to cause physiologic changes—such as increase in anabolic hormones, hypoxia, ROS production, cell swelling, angiogenesis, and mitochondrial biogenesis—that lead to muscle hypertrophy. High-intensity interval training is a type of training that involves all-out effort with high-energy muscle contractions with short rest periods. For resistance training, it has been shown that 70 percent of the one-repetition maximum with ten to twelve repetitions and sixty seconds of rest showed increase in metabolic stress versus using 90 percent of the one-repetition maximum for three to five repetitions and one hundred twenty seconds of rest intervals.[32]

Further, it was determined that muscle hypertrophy increased significantly when resistance training occurred while the muscle had limited oxygen, known as muscle hypoxia. Training during muscle hypoxia created greater hormone release, the recruitment of fast-twitch muscle fibers, cell swelling, and ROS production. This metabolic effect occurred with shorter rest periods, moderate repetitions, and continuous tension on muscles without relaxation, essentially reducing oxygen levels to the muscle.[33]

HIIT principle for resistance training uses moderate to high repetitions (ten to fifteen), short rest intervals (thirty to sixty seconds), training to muscular failure (could not perform another repetition), high intensity muscle contractions (all-out effort), continuous muscle tension, and 70 percent of one-repetition maximum resistance. For example, an assisted pull-up is performed for twelve repetitions at all-out effort. This is followed by a thirty-second break in which another exercise is performed.

HIIT principle for cardiovascular fitness, speed, and quickness uses a three to five training sessions per week model with four to six sets of thirty-second bouts of speed and quickness exercises. These bouts are done with an all-out effort at 100 percent of maximum power, velocity, or maximum heart rate. There is a thirty- to sixty-second rest period between sets. For example, a box quickness drill (sprint, shuffle, back pedal, and sprint, described in detail in future Train 2 Play writings) is done at an all-out effort for thirty seconds. Following the thirty-second drill, the athlete rests for thirty seconds. This drill repeated six times three to five days per week.

The American Academy of Sports Medicine Resistance Training Variables

	Load	Sets	Repetitions	Rest Periods	Frequency
Local Muscle Endurance	Light loads, <30% of 1RM	1–3 per exercise	10–25 or more	1–2 mins for high rep sets (10-25 or more), less than 1 min for 10–15 rep sets	2–3 days/ week for lower level/ untrained, 4–6 days/ week for advanced

	Load	Sets	Repetitions	Rest Periods	Frequency
Strength	60–70% of 1RM for lower level/ untrained, 80–100% for advanced	1–3 per exercise for lower level/ untrained, 4–6 per exercise for advanced	8–12 for lower level/ untrained, 5–8 for advanced	2–3 mins between sets for large muscle group exercises, 1–2 mins for assistance exercises (i.e., bicep curl)	2–3 days/ week for lower level/ untrained, increase based on level of patient
Power	30–60% of 1RM for upper body, 0–60% of 1RM for lower body	1–3 per exercise	3–6	2–3 mins between sets but can do up to 5 mins depending on load	2–3 days/ week for lower level/ untrained, 4–5 days/ week for advanced
Hypertrophy	70–85% of 1RM	1–3 per exercise for lower level/ untrained, 4–6 for advanced	8–12	1–2 mins between sets	2–3 days/ week for lower level/ untrained, 4–5 days/ week for advanced

Adapted from American College of Sports Medicine, "American College of Sports Medicine Position Stand. Progression Models in Resistance Training for Healthy Adults," *Medicine and Science in Sports and Exercise* 41 no. 3 (2009): 687–708.

References

1 Mohamed Souhaiel Chelly et al., "Effects of 8-Week In-Season Plyometric Training on Upper and Lower Limb Performance of Elite Adolescent Handball Players," *Journal of Strength and Conditioning Research* 28 no. 5 (May 2014): 1401–10; Christian Raeder, Jaime Fernandez-Fernandez, andAlexander Ferrauti, "Effects of Six Weeks of Medicine Ball Training on Throwing Velocity, Throwing Precision, and Isokinetic Strength of Shoulder Rotators in Female Handball Players," *Journal of Strength and Conditioning Research* 29 no. 7 (Jul 2015): 1904–1914.

2 Kraemer, "Progression Models in Resistance Training"; T. W. Buford et al., "A Comparison of Periodization Models during Nine Weeks with Equated Volume and Intensity for Strength," *Journal of Strength and Conditioning Research* 21 no. 4 (2007): 1245–1250.

3 William J. Kraemer and Steven Fleck, *Optimizing Strength Training: Designing Nonlinear Periodized Workouts* (Champaign, IL: Human Kinetics, 2007).

4 Ian Jeffreys, *Coaches' Guide to Enhancing Recovery in Athletes: A Multidimensional Approach to Developing a "Performance Lifestyle"* (Monterey, CA: Healthy Learning, 2008).

5 Tudor O. Bompa, G. Gregory Haff, *Periodization: Theory and Methodology of Training*, 5th ed. (Champaign, IL: Human Kinetics, 2008), 191.

6 DeRenne, "Effects of Training Frequency on Strength Maintenance in Pubescent Baseball Players."

7 O. Diallo et al., "Effects of Plyometric Training Followed by a Reduced Training Program on Physical Performance in Prepubescent Soccer Players," *Journal of Sports Medicine and Physical Fitness* 41 (2001): 342–348.

8 Definition of a goal http//en.m.sikipedia.org

9 Jeffreys, *Coaches' Guide to Enhancing Recovery;* Scott Roberts, Traci Ciapponi, and Rebecca Lytle, *Strength Training for Children and Adolescents* (Reston, VA: National Association for Sports and Physical Education, 2008).

10 Chelly et al., "Effects of 8-Week In-Season Plyometric Training."

11 "Joint Actions & Planes of Movement," *PT Direct*, http://www.ptdirect.com/training-design/anatomy-and-physiology/joints-joint-actions-planes-of-movement.

12 "American College of Sports Medicine Position Stand."

13 Bird, Tarpenning, and Marino. "Designing Resistance Training Programmes."; Wayne Westcott et al., "Effects of Regular and Slow Speed Resistance Training on Muscular Strength," *Journal of Sports Medicine and Physical Fitness.* 41 (2001): 154–58; Matthew Rhea and Brandon Alderman, "A Aeta-analysis of

Periodized Versus Nonperiodized Strength and Power Training Programs," *Research Quarterly for Exercise and Sport* 75 (2004): 413–423.

14 "American College of Sports Medicine Position Stand."

15 L. K. Keeler et al., "Early-Phase Adaptations of Traditional Speed vs. Superslow Resistance Training on Strength and Aerobic Capacity in Sedentary Individuals," *Journal of Strength and Conditioning Research* 15 (2001): 309–314.

16 William J. Kraemer, "Involvement of Eccentric Muscle Action May Optimize Adaptations to Resistance Training," *Sport Sci Ex* 4 no. 41 (1992): 230–238.

17 "American College of Sports Medicine Position Stand."

18 Daniel Lorenz et al., "What Performance Characteristics Determine Elite Versus Nonelite Athletes in the Same Sport?" *Sports Health* 5 no. 6 (Nov 2013): 542–547.

19 Aaron Bubbico and Len Kravitz, *Eccentric Training Idea Fitness Journal* 7 (Oct 2010).

20 G. Guilhem and C. Cornu, "Neuromuscular and Muscle-Tendon System Adaptations to Isotonic and Isokinetic Eccentric Exercise," *Annals of Physical and Rehabilitation Medicine* 53 no. 5 (June 2010): 319–341.

21 Jamie Douglas et al., "Eccentric Exercise: Physiological Characteristics and Acute Responses," *Sports Medicine* 47 no. 4 (Sep 2016): 663–675.

22 "American College of Sports Medicine Position Stand."

23 G. J. Davies and T. S. Ellenbecker, "Eccentric Isokinetics," *Orthopaedic Physical Therapy Clinics of North America* 1 no. 2 (1992): 297–336; William Ebben, Christopher Simenz, Randall Jensen, "Evaluation of Plyometric Intensity Using Electromyography," *Journal of Strength and Conditioning Research* 22 no. 3 (2008): 861–868; Erling Asmussen and Flemming Bonde-Petersen, "Storage of Elastic Energy in Skeletal Muscle in Man," *Acta Physiologica Scandinavica* 91 no. 3 (1974): 385–392; C. Bosco and P. V. Komi, "Potentiation of the Mechanical Behavior of the Human Skeletal Muscle through Pre-stretching," *Acta Physiologica Scandinavica*, 106 (1979): 467–472; Eduardo Sáez de Villarreal, Bernardo Requena, and John B. Cronin, "The Effects of Plyometric Training on Sprint Performance: A Meta-Analysis," *Journal of Strength and Conditioning Research* 26 no. 2 (2012): 575–584.

24 Davies and Ellenbecker. "Eccentric Isokinetics."; Ebben, Simenz, and Jensen, "Evaluation of Plyometric Intensity"; Bosco and Komi, "Potentiation of the Mechanical Behavior."

25 Davies and Ellenbecker. "Eccentric Isokinetics."

26 Douglas et al., "Eccentric Exercise."

27 D. W. Robbins, "Postactivation Potentiation and Its Practical Applicability: A Brief Review," *Journal of Strength and Conditioning Research* 19 (2005): 453–458.

28 Artur Golas et al., "Optimizing Post Activation Potentiation for Explosive Activities in Competitive Sports," *Journal of Human Kinetics* 52 (Sep 2016): 95–106.

29 P. M. Cowley, T. Swensen, and G. A. Sforzo, "Efficacy of Instability Resistance Training," *International Journal of Sports Medicine* 28 no. 10 (Oct 2007): 829–35; Erik Zemkova, "Instability Resistance Training for Health and Performance," *Journal of Traditional and Complementary Medicine* 7 no.2 (June 2016): 245–250; James M. Kohler, Sean P. Flanagan, and William C. Whiting, "Muscle Activation Patterns While Lifting Stable and Unstable Loads on Stable and Unstable Surfaces," *Journal of Strength and Conditioning Research* 24 no. 2 (Feb 2010): 313–321; Nils Eckardt, "Lower-Extremity Resistance Training on Unstable Surfaces Improves Proxies of Muscle Strength, Power and Balance in Healthy Older Adults: A Randomised Control Trial," *BMC Geriatrics* 16 no. 1 (Nov 2016): 191.

30 Ahmed Radwan et al., "Is There a Relation between Shoulder Dysfunction and Core Instability?" *International Journal of Sports Physical Therapy* 9 no. 1 (Feb 2014): 8–13.

31 Ibid.

32 Adam M. Gonzalez et al., "Intramuscular Anabolic Signaling and Endocrine Response following High Volume and High Intensity Resistance Exercise Protocols in Trained Men," *Physiol Rep.* 3 no. 7 (2015).

33 Akinobu Nishimura et al., "Hypoxia Increases Muscle Hypertrophy Induced by Resistance Training," *International Journal of Sports Physiology and Performance* 5 (2010): 497–508;

F. B. Favier et al., "HIF-1-Driven Skeletal Muscle Adaptations to Chronic Hypoxia: Molecular Insights into Muscle Physiology," *Cellular and Molecular Life Sciences* 72 no. 24 (2015): 4681–4696.

CHAPTER 5

Basic Concepts of Exercise

In this chapter I will discuss many of the terms and ideas that are integral to exercise and are often confused by coaches and trainers. Knowledge of these training definitions will not only help you understand the ideas behind the Train 2 Play methods but also exercise in general. These fundamental concepts will also help the athlete optimize his or her training effect.

Metabolic Stress

Our bodies have the amazing ability to adapt to environmental and physical stressors. This adaptation process is critical to the long-term evolutionary success of our species. In the exercise world we can use this adaptation process to enhance physical performance. During certain types of exercise, our bodies go through metabolic stress. During intense resistance exercise, our bodies move towards a low energy state. This low energy state leads to the accumulation of metabolites (lactate, phosphate, and hydrogen ions), the byproduct of normal muscle metabolism. These metabolites in the blood trigger key processes that are essential for the development and adaptation of muscle, such as hormonal release (growth hormone, testosterone, and insulin-releasing growth factor), cell swelling, and reactive oxygen species (ROS). The right type of training will also cause the development of mitochondria (the energy powerhouse of the cell) and increase blood vessel development (angiogenesis), which are key factors in the development of muscle.[1] The right balance between intensity, volume, and rest and recovery can optimize the use of metabolic stress in the physical development of the human body.

Repetition

A repetition, often referred to as a rep, is the execution of one complete movement. For example, a squat is done ten consecutive times before a rest. Each squat movement is a repetition. A simple way to establish the repetition range is by using trial and error to determine the maximum load that can be handled for the prescribed exercise. For example, a child or adolescent may begin with no resistance performing one or two sets of ten to fifteen repetitions, focusing on the appropriate movement pattern or exercise technique, then progressing to loaded. Once load is added, it is essential that the exercise technique and movement pattern be preserved without movement error. The repetitions will vary depending on the goal of the exercise. For example, plyometric exercises are designed to create power and must be performed with maximum intensity and effort. In this case, fewer repetitions need to be performed, typically only three to five, to keep the high level of muscular effort. In order to create muscle strength, more repetitions, typically ten to twelve, need to be performed with moderate load.[2]

Repetition Velocity

The velocity, or speed, at which an exercise is performed can affect the specific musculoskeletal adaptations to a training program. In the Train 2 Play method, the individual must first learn how to perform each movement pattern and exercise correctly with no load at low velocity. However, once the movement pattern is learned, the training velocities may be used to replicate the specifics of the sport. For example, in order to replicate the baseball swing, a medicine ball plyometric rotational exercise can be used. In order to replicate the sequencing and explosiveness of the swing, the repetition velocity of the exercise must be fast just like the swing. On the other hand, the box step-up exercise may emphasize the eccentric phase of the movement. In this case the repetition velocity is slow, bending the knee and lowering to a count of five seconds.[3] The performance of different training velocities will be utilized to optimize the training effect and to create overload.[4]

Intensity

Intensity is the effort at which a drill or exercise is performed. In simple terms, this is how easy or difficult a particular activity is to perform. Intensity can be measured in terms of power (work performed per unit of time). In the Train 2 Play method, all concentric muscle contractions should be performed with a high level of intensity, making the exercise as challenging as the athlete can handle. Key training verbiage that may help the athlete with the intensity are "explode" or "fire" through the movement.

Set

A set is an exercise with a rest interval. For example, ten squats followed by a rest is an example of one set of the exercise. As early as 1948, DeLorme, a rehabilitation expert who used strength training to help children recover from illnesses, recommended the use of heavy resistance and low repetitions during sets to develop strength and light resistance with high repetitions to develop muscular endurance. Three sets of ten repetitions maximum (RM) with progressive loading during each set was proposed to develop strength. Conversely, the Oxford technique uses a regressive loading model for resistance exercise. The programs share similarities: rest periods and increases in resistance over time. The DeLorme technique starts out with less weight and adds weight while maintaining ten repetitions, building a warm-up into the protocol. The Oxford technique starts at the ten repetitions and removes weight, decreasing the resistance progressively as fatigue occurs.[5]

In a randomized prospective study, the DeLorme and Oxford techniques were compared for training efficacy over a nine-week training period. The DeLorme technique was more effective for a 10RM increase, although the differences were not statistically significant.[6]

Volume Load

The volume load is the total quantity of exercises performed during a workout. For example, eight exercises performed at three sets of ten reps would give a total volume load of 240 reps.

Rest Period/Recovery Period

The rest period is the time of rest between each set. This is based on the metabolic demands and the complexity of the exercise. Complete metabolic muscle recovery occurs within two to three minutes. Complete neurological (nervous system) recovery takes five to ten minutes. Studies have shown that children and adolescents are able to recover from high-intensity, short-term, intermittent exercise faster than adults.[7]

The recovery should be set on an individual basis, taking into account the athlete's response to the activity. Based on the evidence that adolescents can resist fatigue to a greater extent than adults during several repeated sets of resistance exercise, a shorter rest interval (about sixty to ninety seconds) may suffice when performing a moderate-intensity resistance exercise protocol.

However, training intensity, training volume, exercise choice, and the individual's fitness level will influence the length of the rest interval. When performing our plyometric and/or speed and agility workouts, which require higher levels of power or skill, longer rest intervals between sets, perhaps two to three minutes, may be needed.[8]

Rest and recovery between training sessions will be discussed in great detail in a subsequent chapter; however, forty-eight to seventy-two hours between high-intensity strength and power training should be provided to allow for adequate regeneration times and therefore maximal stimulus intensities in training.[9]

In the Train 2 Play method, we use an alternate exercise program in which multiple exercises of different muscle groups are done in order to optimize time and efficiency as well as improve cardiovascular fitness.

Frequency

Frequency is the number of training sessions per week. Young athletes should perform our training two times per week in the off-season and one time per week during the season. Frequency ultimately depends on the volume and load of exercises, the type of movement (concentric, eccentric, isometric, or plyometric) during the workout, the training level of the athlete, and the goals of training. Frequency of training sessions has been found to be effective at two to three days a week in the untrained and one to two days a week for maintenance.

A research study of boys and girls aged seven to twelve compared the effects of one versus two days per week of strength training. The authors found greater muscular strength gains when the exercise routine was performed twice per week as opposed to once per week. Interestingly, there were no injuries or adverse reactions to the exercise participants, lending to the evidence that it is safe to perform strength training in young children.[10]

In a systematic research review, it was found that training two times per week promoted superior muscle development versus training one time per week.[11] At the current time, there is no available research to state that training a given muscle group more than two times per week has any added benefits. Being that the body needs adequate rest and recovery, training greater that two times per week for a given muscle group may even be detrimental to physical development and performance.

The American College of Sports Medicine's position statement on frequency of training is as follows: "The recommendation for training frequency is 2-3 days per week for novice training, 3-4 days per week for intermediate training, and 4-5 days per week for advanced training."[12]

References

1 Marcelo Conrado de Freitas et al., "Role of Metabolic Stress for Enhancing Muscle Adaptations: Practical Applications," *World Journal of Methodology* 7 no. 2 (2017): 46–54.

2 American College of Sports Medicine, "American College of Sports Medicine Position Stand. Progression Models in Resistance Training for Healthy Adults," *Medicine and Science in Sports and Exercise* 41 no. 3 (2009): 687–708.

3 Stephen P. Bird, Kyle M. Tarpenning, and Frank E. Marino. "Designing Resistance Training Programmes to Enhance Muscular Fitness: A Review of Acute Programme Variables," *Sports Med* 35 no. 10 (2005): 841–851.

4 William J. Kraemer et al., "Progression Models in Resistance Training for Healthy Adults." *Medicine and Science in Sports and Exercise* 34 (2002): 364–380.

5 Thomas L. DeLorme, "Restoration of Muscle Power by Heavy Resistance Exercise," *Journal of Bone & Joint Surgery* 27 (1945): 645–667.

6 David E. Fish et al., "Optimal Resistance Training: Comparison of DeLorme with Oxford Techniques," *American Journal of Physical Medicine and Rehabilitation* 82 no. 12 (2003): 903–909.

7 Kraemer, "Progression Models in Resistance Training."

8 Andreas Zafeiridis et al., "Recovery during High-Intensity Intermittent Anaerobic Exercise in Boys, Teens and Men," *Medicine and Science in Sports and Exercise* 37 (2005): 505–512; José M. C. Soares et al., "Children Are Less Susceptible to Exercise-Induced Muscle Damage than Adults: A Preliminary Investigation," *Pediatric Exercise Science* 8 (1996): 361–367; Avery D. Faigenbaum et al., "Effect of Rest Interval Length on Bench Press Performance in Boys, Teens and Men," *Pediatric Exercise Science* 20 (2008): 457–469.

9 Steven J. Fleck "Non-Linear Periodization for General Fitness & Athletes," *Journal of Human Kinetics* 29A (Sep 2011): 41–45.

10 Avery D. Faigenbaum et al., "Comparison of 1 and 2 Days per Week of Strength Training in Children," *Research Quarterly for Exercise and Sport* 73 no. 4 (2002): 416–424.

11 Menno Henselmans and Brad J. Schoenfeld, "The Effect of Inter-Set Rest Intervals on Resistance Exercise-Induced Muscle Hypertrophy." *Sports Medicine* 44 no. 12 (Dec 2014):1635–1643.

12 "American College of Sports Medicine Position Stand."

CHAPTER 6

The Power of Muscle: Function, Performance, and Genetics

Understanding muscle and how it functions can be important in creating the right exercise program to meet the demands of the sport. The term *muscle* is derived from the Latin *musculus*, meaning "little mouse," speculated to be due to the fact that contracting muscle looks like mice moving under the skin.[1]

Muscle cells contain protein filaments of actin, myosin, and titin. Actin and myosin slide past each other, shortening the length of the cell during the muscle contraction. Titin is considered a ridged backbone that binds the actin and myosin, enhancing the force of the contraction. An in-depth study of muscle function is beyond the scope of this writing. For more information on muscle function go to http://muscle.ucsd.edu/musintro/bridge.shtml. In this chapter we will cover some of the basics of muscle function that are used for training and athletic performance. While some of it may sound complicated, it is only scratching the surface of the intricate workings inside the body.

Muscle Fibers

Muscles function to produce force and motion. In order for a muscle to contract to produce force, it needs adenosine triphosphate (ATP), which is a form of energy from the breakdown of carbohydrates and fats.

Amino acids, the "building blocks" of life, are essential for body functions of organs, glands, and the cardiovascular system. They are essential for the repair and healing of damaged tissue, such as muscle, bone, skin, and hair. Amino acids build protein, which creates muscle development.[2]

Muscle has specific contractile properties that are closely related to human function and performance. Muscle fiber types can be broken down into two main types: slow twitch (type I) and fast twitch (type II). Fast-twitch muscle fibers are further divided into type IIa (fast-twitch oxidative) and type IIb (fast-twitch glycolytic). Type IIa falls between type I and type IIb.

The recruitment or "firing" of muscle fiber activity follows an orderly pattern based on muscle size and intensity of effort. Slow-twitch fibers are typically recruited at low-intensity efforts, meaning less than 30 percent intensity. As the intensity of the muscle activity increases, the fast-twitch type IIa fibers are recruited. The recruitment of fast-twitch type IIa fibers occurs between 30 percent and 80 percent of maximal intensity. At greater than 80 percent muscle activity intensity, the fast-twitch IIb fibers are recruited. In order to optimally develop power, the exercise intensity level needs to be above 80 percent.[3]

For example, a basketball player during a game is jogging, dribbling the ball upcourt. He or she is primarily using slow-twitch muscle. As the player sees an opening to the basket, he or she begins to sprint to the basket. Fast-twitch type IIa muscle fibers are being utilized. The player next explodes to the basket, jumping to make a layup. That explosive effort uses the fast-twitch type IIb muscle fibers.

Fast-twitch type IIb muscle produces the most power (force and speed) due to its large size, but it has the least potential for endurance activities. As far as time, type IIb fiber is predominately used in zero to ten-second duration high-intensity efforts. Fast-twitch type IIa fiber is most active in the fifteen to thirty-second range. Keep in mind that the effort intensity must be greater than 30 percent to elicit the fast-twitch muscle contraction. Slow-twitch muscle is used exclusively once the work period is greater than thirty to sixty seconds at low intensity levels. For example, slow-twitch muscle would be used for endurance activities such as a 5K run. Fast-twitch muscle activity would involve intense, high-force activities such as jumping, sprinting, throwing, hitting, striking, and kicking. In order to create the greatest gains in exercise training, it is essential to be specific to the type of muscle contraction used in the athlete's sport.

Muscle Fiber Type Characteristics

Property	Type I	Type IIa	Type IIb
Fiber color	Red	White	White
Motor Neuron Size	Small	Large	Largest
CaATPase isoform	Slow	Fast	Fastest
Time to Peak Tension	Slow	Fast	Fastest
Time to Relaxation	Slow	Fast	Fastest
Oxidative Capacity	High	Medium	Low
Myoglobin Content	Highest	High	Low
Glycolytic Capacity	Low	High	Highest
Glycogen Content	Low	High	High
Capillary Density	High	High	Low
Mitochondrial	High	Medium	Low

Adapted from W. J. Kraemer et al., "Compatibility of High-Intensity Strength and Endurance Training on Hormonal and Skeletal Muscle Adaptations," *Journal of Applied Physiology* 78 no. 3 (1995): 976–989; G. J. Bell et al., "Effect of Concurrent Strength and Endurance Training on Skeletal Muscle Properties and Hormone Concentrations in Humans," *European Journal of Applies Physiology* 81 no. 5 (2000): 418–427.

Conversion of muscle fiber to fast twitch

There is some evidence to support the fact that muscle fibers can change typing based on the training demands. In recent studies, it was demonstrated that strength and power exercise programs could cause some increase in fast-twitch fibers, suggesting that specific power training may lead to muscle fiber conversions.[4]

In our young athletes who play sports that require power, speed, and agility, we want as much muscle fiber adaptation as possible to meet the specific demands of their sports. For example, baseball hitting and throwing requires a fast-twitch response. The faster one can get the bat through the strike zone or one's arm through the throwing zone, the greater the ball speed. In this example we would want a portion of our training to be ballistic and explosive in nature to preferentially train the fast-twitch muscle and hope to cause increased fast-twitch muscle adaptations.

Genetics and muscle type

Many people believe that athletes are born with power and speed with limited ability to improve with training. "You either have it or you don't," they say, so most athletes spend little time on power and speed training. Genetics certainly play a role in the athlete's speed and power. All humans have a mix of slow- and fast-twitch muscle.[5] However, the type of muscle fiber an athlete predominately has can be important to his or her success in a given sport.

Scientists have discovered a variation in a gene called *ACTN3* (alpha-actin-3 R577X polymorphism), the "gene for speed." The *ACTN3* gene encodes a protein present in fast-twitch muscle fibers. One hundred percent of Olympic sprinters have *ACTN3*. Nearly 40 percent of the population has a mutation in this gene and does not produce the protein. Thereby, these individuals have less fast-twitch muscle fiber content and a predominance of slow-twitch muscle fiber. Slow-twitch muscle fiber has characteristics that enhance endurance-type activities.[6]

On the other hand, a study looking at *AGTR2* gene C allele, the gene involved in skeletal muscle development, associated this allele with an increased proportion of slow-twitch muscle fibers. In the study, the athletes with this gene were endurance athletes with high levels of aerobic performance. If the individual had the A allele of this gene, they had a higher percentage of fast-twitch fibers and power-oriented disciplines.[7]

In a study looking at type II fast-twitch muscle fibers, it was determined that 30 percent of type II fibers could be explained exclusively by differences in the local environment and level of muscular contractile activity.[8] Therefore, independent of one's genetics, there is opportunity to increase fast-twitch muscle. This is where proper training at certain developmental time periods is critical to development of fast-twitch muscle.

While the study of the human genome and genetics is in its infancy, with thousands of interacting genes that may influence the athlete's development, research has shown that with the appropriate training program, athletes can increase their speed and power independent of their genetics. Now, these individuals may not be able to hit a baseball four hundred feet or run a sub-nine-second hundred-meter dash, but they can optimize their genetics. For the individual who does have *ACTN3, AGTR2* gene A allele, and possibly a myriad of other genes, his or her potential to be a powerful, explosive, ballistic athlete is much greater and could truly be optimized through proper training. One can be a great athlete without the *ACTN3* gene; however, he or she most likely will not be an Olympic sprinter.

In the Train 2 Play Sports training method, we use the knowledge of the muscle physiology to create functional movements and exercises that are specific to the sport, giving the individual the best opportunity to develop the body to enhance motor skill and sports performance.

Core and Spinal Stabilization

Stabilization occurs when a large number of muscle groups contract against one another to hold the body in place so that other portions can push or pull against this stable base to cause movement. This is done through an isometric contraction. Most of the important stabilization in the body happens in the torso, lumbar spine, pelvis, and the scapula (shoulder blade). As you'll recall, this was described in chapter 4.

Flexibility and Stretching

Flexibility is the absolute gross range of motion for a joint. There are many anatomical factors that affect flexibility such as joint capsule, ligaments, muscle, tendon, fascia (covering of muscle), and neural structures interacting together.

Increased flexibility does not necessarily lead to increased performance and injury prevention. In some cases, increased flexibility may actually decrease performance and lead to injury. Some studies have shown that increased flexibility beyond what is needed in the sport or activity may contribute to injury, creating hypermobility (increase in normal joint range of motion).[9]

From a clinical perspective, symmetry of flexibility from side to side in a given region of the body is critical for performance and injury prevention. For example, a tight hamstring on one side may lead to asymmetrical loading on one side of the body, potentially leading to knee, hip, or lower back pain. Another example is limited internal rotation of the shoulder in throwing athletes, known as glenohumeral internal rotation deficit, or GIRD. This asymmetry between internal and external rotation of the shoulder potentially leads to altered stress and force, leading to shoulder injury.[10] More research is needed in this area, but the general wisdom is that athletes should not have asymmetry from side to side.

Stretching prior to working out: dynamic warm-up versus static stretching

Dynamic stretching is a rhythmic, smooth, continuous series of movements that stretches many joints of the body in functional patterns and can increase power, flexibility, and range of motion. If done prior to a workout or an athletic endeavor, this movement-based warm-up has been shown to improve performance and prevent injury. Static stretching, the traditional thirty-second hold variety, has long been the standard activity performed prior to athletic events.

Static stretching prior to an activity may even have adverse effects, such as calming the athlete, decreasing blood flow, and reducing overall strength output. Furthermore, there is a neuromuscular inhibitory response to static stretching. The stretched muscle becomes less responsive and stays weakened for up to sixty minutes after stretching, which is not how an athlete wants to begin competition. The muscle is then actually weaker and may be more vulnerable to injury. Conversely, research has shown that dynamic stretching, unlike static stretching, does not cause the inhibitory response to the nervous system. Beyond this, dynamic stretching will increase heart and respiratory rates, allowing the athlete to be better prepared for activity. Dynamic stretching also primes the body for the more intense activity that is to come.

A study comparing hamstring strength production during a leg curl exercise performed after both static and dynamic stretching revealed significant differences in strength output. Results showed that static stretching produced a significant reduction in hamstring strength for a time period lasting up to one hour post-stretching. Dynamic stretching, however, resulted in significantly higher muscle temperature and increased muscle flexibility. This study supports the use of dynamic stretching prior to a competition or training session and suggests that static stretching be used as a post-workout cool-down.[11]

The right warm-up should accomplish two things: loosen muscles and tendons to increase the range of motion of various joints and, literally, warm up the body. When you're at rest, there is less blood flow to muscles and tendons and they stiffen. A well-designed warm-up starts by increasing body heat and blood flow. Warm muscles and dilated blood vessels pull oxygen from the bloodstream more efficiently and use stored muscle fuel more effectively.

The optimal way to warm up and stretch prior to an athletic event is to start with a few minutes of low-intensity aerobic exercise, like walking or jogging around the court or field. Follow this by performing dynamic stretches, such as walking lunges, body weight squats, high knee hugs, lateral lunge walks, straight leg marching, quad walks, and arm circles for thirty seconds to one minute. Static stretching can simply be moved to end of the workout. Don't trash it altogether, because the inhibitory effect on the nervous system can be beneficial to elongate tight muscles, reduce soreness, and speed recovery.

The benefits of a dynamic warm-up on performance are summed up below:

- Elevated muscle temperature due to increased circulation increases joint range of motion.
- Elevated tissue temperatures enable warm muscles to contract with more force and at a faster rate.

- Improved oxygen-carbon dioxide exchange leads to more available oxygen.
- Blood flow to the heart and muscles increases.
- Hormonal activity is enhanced.
- Increased synovial fluid in the joints decreases the viscosity, helping joints move better.
- Muscles become more pliable, decreasing muscle damage and leading to less delayed-onset muscle soreness.
- Muscular coordination of movement increases with better motor skill.
- Cardiovascular strength and work capacity increases.
- Psychological focus and attention increases.[12]

Static stretching

Static stretching should be done following one's workout. Flexibility decreases with age, but it can be increased across all groups by performing static stretches. Joint range of motion is improved after flexibility training is performed two to three times per week for three to four weeks. Stretches should be held for thirty seconds and repeated two to four times, with enhanced range of motion occurring over three to twelve weeks. Flexibility is most effective when the muscle temperature is elevated with light cardiovascular exercise. Although flexibility exercises are commonly performed, no consistent links have shown a reduction in injuries. While static stretching has historically been performed prior to activity, more evidence is suggesting that dynamic flexibility is a better choice prior to performance activities and that static stretching should be performed after activity.[13]

References

1 Alfred Carey Carpenter (2007). "Muscle." *Anatomy Words.* Retrieved 3 October 2012 Douglas Harper (2012). "Muscle." *Online Etymology Dictionary.* Retrieved 3 October 2012.

2 "Amino Acid," *Wikipedia*, https://en.wikipedia.org/wiki/Amino_acid.

3 George Davies, Bryan Riemann, and Robert Manske, "Current Concepts of Plyometric Exercise," *International Journal of Sports Physical Therapy* 10 no. 6 (Nov 2015): 760–786.

4 R. S. Staron et al., "Muscle Hypertrophy and Fast Fiber Type Conversions in Heavy Resistance-Trained Women," *European Journal of Applied Physiology and Occupational Physiology* 60 (1990).

5 Andrew C. Fry, "The Role of Resistance Exercise Intensity on Muscle Fibre Adaptations," *Sports Medicine* 34 no. 10 (Aug 2004): 663–679; Gerson E. Campos et al., "Muscular Adaptations in Response to Three Different Resistance-Training Regimens: Specificity of Repetition Maximum Training Zones," *European Journal of Applied Physiology* 88 no. 1–2 (November 2002): 50–60.

6 Leysan J. Mustafina et al., "AGTR2 Gene Polymorphism Is Associated with Muscle Fibre Composition, Athletic Status and Aerobic Performance," *Experimental Physiology* 99 (Aug 2014): 1042–1052.

7 Ibid.; David G. Behm et al., "Relationship between Hockey Skating Speed and Selected Performance Measures," *Journal of Strength and Conditioning Research* 19 (2005): 326–331.

8 J. A. Simoneau and C. Bouchard, "Genetic Determinism of Fiber Type Proportion in Human Skeletal Muscle," *The FASEB Journal* 9 no. 11 (Aug 1995): 1091–1095.

9 Paul Hodges et al., "Changes in the Mechanical Properties of the Trunk in Low Back Pain May Be Associated with Recurrence," *Journal of Biomechanics* 42 no. 1 (2006): 61–66.

10 Kevin E. Wilk et al., "Correlation of Glenohumeral Internal Rotation Deficit and Total Rotational Motion to Shoulder Injuries in Professional Baseball Pitchers," *Physical Therapy* 85 no. 11 (2005):1201–1207.

11 Michael J. Duncan and Lorayne Woodfield, "Acute Effects of Warm Up Protocol on Flexibility and Vertical Jump in Children," *Journal of Exercise Physiology Online* (2006).

12 F. G. Shellock, "Physiological, Psychological, and Injury Prevention Aspects of Warm Up," *National Strength and Conditioning Association Journal* 8 no. 5 (1986): 24–27; Andrea J. Fradkin, Tsharni R. Zazryn, and James M. Smoliga,

"Effects of Warming-Up on Physical Performance: A Systematic Review with Meta-Analysis," *Journal of Strength and Conditioning Research,* 24 no. 1 (2008): 140–148.

13 Ann Fredrick A and Christopher Fredrick, *Stretch to Win*. (Champaign, IL: Human Kinetics, 2006); W. D. Bandy, J. M. Irion, and M. Briggler, "The Effect of Time and Frequency of Static Stretching on Flexibility of the Hamstring Muscles," *Physical Therapy* 77 (1997): 1090–1096.

CHAPTER 7

Adolescent Growth Spurt/Peak Height Velocity

Peak height velocity (PHV) is the period of time in which an adolescent experiences his or her fastest upward growth in stature, better known as a growth spurt. During the adolescent growth spurt, the average male typically achieves a PHV of approximately 3.27 inches and the female 3.07 inches. The range for males is 2.28 inches to 5.16 inches and for females is 2.13 inches to 4.41 inches.[1]

Approximately two years prior to the adolescent growth spurt is the onset of puberty. This occurs around thirteen years of age in males and eleven years of age in females. The onset of puberty coincides with the body's release of a variety of hormones such as growth hormone, thyroxine, insulin, and corticosteroids, all of which influence growth rate; leptin, which alters body composition; and parathyroid hormone, 1,25-dihydroxy-vitamin D, and calcitonin, all of which affect skeletal mineralization. However, the key hormone in growth is growth hormone. This is mediated by growth hormone–releasing hormone (GHRH) and somatostatin that are released from the pituitary gland of the brain.[2]

During this rapid release of hormones, the young athlete can see significant increases in athletic skill and sports performance. The hormones will increase muscular development, thereby allowing the athlete to improve in strength, speed, agility, power, and explosiveness.[3]

Before, during, and after PHV, windows of opportunity develop in which the athlete is reaching an optimal time period for exercise training. If this window of opportunity is missed, the athlete may not reach his or her full physical potential. Those who train during this window will have greater opportunities to reach greater athletic development and skill.[4]

What Type of Training Is Best during Puberty to Optimize Physical Development?

The type of training utilized during adolescent puberty is critical for optimal physical development. In thirty-three out of thirty-four research studies on resistance exercise training in untrained adolescent athletes, there were marked increases in muscular strength and power. The power improvements were demonstrated in movements such as vertical jump, upper extremity power, and sprint performance, all of which lent to improvements in sports performance.[5]

Resistance training using free weights has been shown to be better than exercise machines due to greater muscular activity to balance and control the weight, greater range of motion, and the ability to create sports-specific movements. Resistance training programs using free weights consistently enhanced muscular strength and agility versus other exercise devices such as machines.[6]

At PHV, in order to optimize this window of physical development, it is imperative to use resistance training in combination with plyometrics. There is a specific type of combined training that will meet the exact needs of the hormonally developing athlete, known as complex training or post-activation potential.

In research studies, complex training programs had the greatest crossover to improve sports-specific performance. Complex training provides a wide variety of training variables, such as slow, heavy strength exercises with light, fast, explosive exercises. These types of programs can utilize all planes of motion with a variety of contraction types, making it ideal to enhance sports performance. An example of complex training would be to perform a heavy back squat for three or four repetitions, followed by a set of five explosive jumps. Studies show that loads of 80–90 percent of the one-repetition maximum were most beneficial in terms of improving muscle strength in adolescent athletes. This means performing fewer repetitions with higher weight and greater intensity levels.[7]

In all of the studies presented, there were very few injuries. The American College of Sports Medicine concluded that resistance training is safe for children and adolescents if appropriately prescribed and supervised.[8]

How Do You Know When an Adolescent Is in the Peak Height Velocity Stage?

Peak height velocity can be predicted in a number of ways, from genital assessment to X-rays of the hand. There is a simple, noninvasive method of predicting physical maturity using gender, date of birth, date of measurement, standing height (cm), sitting height (cm), and weight (kg). In a research study, it has been shown to be a reliable test.[9] Robert Mirwald and his colleagues at the College of Kinesiology at the University of Saskatchewan have developed a website in which an individual can put in the vital information and get their predicted biological maturity level. This can be found at https://kinesiology.usask.ca/growthutility/phv_ui.php.

Knowing the biological maturity level can help the physical therapist, trainer, parent, or coach to progress the individual's strength and conditioning program to meet the athlete's physical conditioning windows of opportunity. As mentioned previously, independent of age, a periodized training program is essential to attain an optimal physiological training effect. As the athlete moves toward puberty, complex training programs can be instituted to take advantage of the body's natural growth and development hormones, which will allow for the development of muscle mass, strength, and power.

References

1 Rhodri S. Lloyd and Jon L. Oliver, "The Youth Physical Development Model: A New Approach to Long-Term Athletic Development," *Strength and Conditioning Journal* 34 no. 3 (2012): 61–72; Growth Charts – Data Table of Stature-for-age Charts. 2001; Alan D. Rogol, Pamela A. Clark, and James N. Roemmich, "Growth and Pubertal Development in Children and Adolescents: Effects of Diet and Physical Activity. *American Journal of Clinical Nutrition* 72 no. S2 (Aug 2000): 521S–8S; Gaston Beunen and Robert Malina, "Growth and Physical Performance Relative to the Timing of the Adolescent Spurt," *Exercise and Sport Science Review* 16 (1988): 503–540.

2 Alex Hannaman, *Adolescent Health Care: A Practical Guide* 4th ed. (Lippincott Williams & Wilkins, 2003); G. D. Myer et al., "When to Initiate Integrative Neuromuscular Training to Reduce Sport-Related Injuries and Enhance Health in Youth," *Current Sports Medicine Reports* 10 (2011): 157–166; P. Ford et al., "The Long-Term Athlete Development Model: Physiological Evidence and Application," *Journal of Sports Sciences,* 29 no. 4 (2011), 389–402.

3 Alanna Martin et al., "Possible Hormone Predictors of Physical Performance in Adolescent Team Sport Athletes," *Journal of Strength and Conditioning Research* (May 2017); Rogol, Clark, and Roemmich, "Growth and Pubertal Development."

4 Istvan Balyi and Ann Hamilton, *Long-Term Athlete Development: Trainability in Childhood and Adolescence—Windows of Opportunity, Optimal Trainability,* (Victoria, Canada: National Coaching Institute British Columbia & Advanced Training and Performance Ltd, 2004); M. C. Rumpf et al., "Effect of Different Training Methods on Running Sprint Times in Male Youth," *Pediatric Exercise Science* (2012); Robert Malina, Claude Bouchard, and Oded Bar-Or, *Growth, Maturation, and Physical Activity*. (Champaign, IL: Human Kinetics, 2004).

5 Simon K. Harries, David R. Lubans, Robin Callister, "Resistance Training to Improve Power and Sports Performance in Adolescent Athletes: A Systematic Review and Meta-Analysis," *Journal of Science and Medicine in Sport* 15 no. 6 (2012): 532–40.

6 Malina, "Weight Training in Youth-Growth."; Robert L. Mirwald et al., "An Assessment of Maturity from Anthropometric Measurements," *Medicine and Science Sports Exercise,* 34 no. 4 (2002): 689–694; Avery D. Faigenbaum et al., "Youth Resistance Training: Updated Position Statement Paper from the National Strength and Conditioning Association," *Journal of Strength and Conditioning Research* 23 no. S5 (Aug 2009): S60–79.

7 William Ebben, "Complex Training: A Brief Review," *Journal of Science and Medicine in Sport* 2 (June 2002): 42–46.

8 Katherine Stabenow Dahab and Teri Metcalf McCambridge, "Strength Training in Children and Adolescents: Raising the Bar for Young Athletes?" *Sports Health* 1 no. 3 (May 2009): 223–226.

9 Robert M. Malina, "Skeletal Age and Age Verification in Youth Sport," *Sports Medicine*, 41 (2011): 925–47.

CHAPTER 8

Overload and Optimal Rest and Recovery to Optimize Sports Performance

In order to create the best physical adaptations to training, there must be a careful balance between training dose and recovery. After overload training or competition, it is essential to have a recovery phase that returns the body to its balance or set point, known as homeostasis. This recovery is done through active rest, passive rest, and nutrition.

The greater the physical stress on the body, the longer the recovery time needed.[1] It is during the rest and recovery phase that physiological adaptations occur, allowing the athlete to see gains in strength, power, speed, agility, quickness, and endurance. There are four phases of physical training that can help the athlete optimize the training effect: shock, resistance, supercompensation, and physical adaptation.

Positive Adaptation to Physical Training and Overload

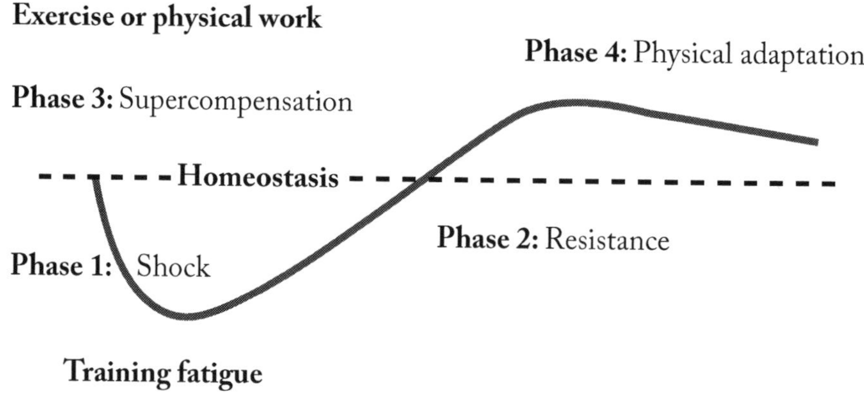

Adapted from H. Selye, 1956. *The Stress of Life* (London: Longmans Green).

What Happens to the Body during Exercise or Competition?

Phase 1 of training: shock

As the exercise or competition begins, there is a physiological shock to the body. The physiological response can be accelerated heart rate, rapid respiration, increased circulation, increased muscular effort, enhanced neurological activity, or other physiological responses. If there is sufficient volume and intensity during training or competition, overload of the body systems and tissues will occur. This overload stresses the body, leading to training fatigue and microtrauma to the body tissues. The overexertion during training takes the body away from its homeostasis, progressing to a fatigue state.

Phase 2 of training: resistance

As the body is stressed during the activity, it tries to resist the fatigue by attempting to return to its physiological baseline or set point. The body's attempt to resist fatigue leads to a greater physiological adaptation above the previous baseline set point. After the vigorous activity, the positive physical adaptations due to training and competition occur during passive rest (sleep and sedentary activities) and active rest (stretching, good nutrition, massage, manipulation, foam rolling, and so on). This resting process allows the body to recover and prepare for the next training or competition as described above. This physiological movement above the body's baseline set point following a workout or intense competition is called the supercompensation phase, or the resistance response.

Phase 3 of training: supercompensation

In the supercompensation phase, the body's organs and tissues are recovered physiologically from the workout or competition. The body systems are primed and ready to make physiological adaptations and changes. These changes could be in muscle hypertrophy, muscle strength and endurance, cardiorespiratory fitness, and other body adaptations. The supercompensation phase is the ideal time for the next workout or competition in that given week. The previous workout or competition acts as a springboard to physical development and adaptation. Essentially, the body is stacking the benefits of the previous workout onto the current training.

Finding the right timing for the next workout to utilize the supercompensation phase can be difficult. The supercompensation phase is typically from one to four days following the initial workout or competition. This phase is dependent on the athlete's physical conditioning, genetics, volume of workload (time, repetitions, sets, and number of exercises), and/or previous injury. If the next training bout occurs after the supercompensation phase, less physiological adaptation will occur as the body has returned to its original baseline. Conversely, if the next training occurs during the supercompensation phase, the athlete will have greater potential for physiological adaptations, such as gains in strength, speed, power, endurance, and agility.

In order to determine the right time to start the second workout or competition, the individual must "listen" to his or her body. All soreness, including DOMS (delayed-onset muscle soreness due to lactic acid buildup), tightness, stiffness, and fatigue should be gone. The next workout should be done soon after the athlete's body feels recovered and rested.

Phase 4 of training: physical adaptation

After six to twelve weeks of cyclical overloading of the body along with adequate rest and recovery, signs of physical adaptations will be apparent. Continuing the training over months and years can lead to significant positive bodily and functional changes. These physical adaptations will be specific to the physical demand placed on the body during training (remember the SAID principle—specific adaptation to imposed demand). For example, if the athlete trains for endurance, there will be specific adaptations in endurance. If the athlete trains for explosive power and speed, the body will respond by creating adaptations to enhance power and speed.

The bottom line is, the appropriate training plus adequate recovery time equals specific desired physiological adaptations. If this is done with appropriate timing, physiological gains can be multiplied from the pre-workout status. This is why physical fitness gains will only occur with structured, consistent, long-term training.[2]

When starting a workout training program, the athlete should start out with two to three training days per week with twenty-four to forty-eight hours between workouts. The volume (number of exercises, repetitions, and sets) and load (weight of resistance) should match the physical state of the athlete beginning training. Typically, one to three sets of eight to fifteen repetitions can be used for the beginning level or novice athlete. Over time, the athlete can progress based on his or her physical response to training. One of the most common training errors in the beginner is too much volume or intensity of workout.

Overuse and Injury

Negative adaptation to physical overtraining and overload

Physical work or exercise

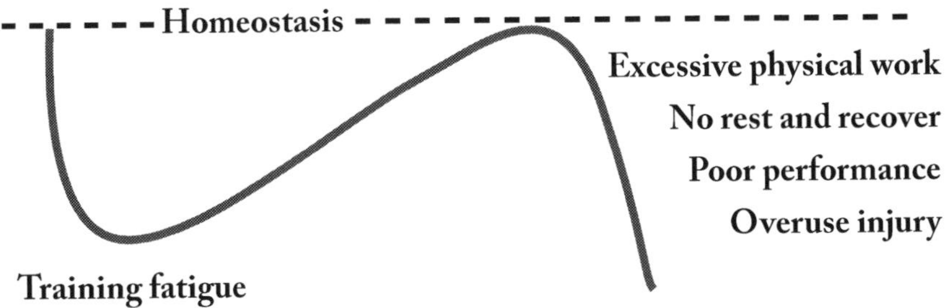

Adapted from H. Selye, *The Stress of Life* (London: Longmans Green, 1956).

If there are excessive workouts, games, or competitions without adequate rest and recovery, the body will be overused and will not return to its balance point, leading to negative physical adaptations.

With overuse, the fatigue and microtrauma created eventually leads to macrotrauma, injury (muscle strains, ligament tears, stress fractures, growth plate injuries, etc.), and pain. Minimally, overuse leads to a reduction in the training effects and physical development, meaning there will be a reduction in speed, power, strength, endurance, quickness, balance, motor control, concentration, and so on. Consequently, the negative physical adaptations lead to poor athletic performance.

Without adequate rest and recovery there will be excessive fatigue, physiological breakdown, and inhibition of the body's healing and recovery processes. The inadequate healing leads to overuse injuries and/or burnout. Thus, competition and training errors are the most common cause of overuse injuries. The following are risk factors for overuse injuries:

- higher training volumes
- overscheduling (multiple competitive events in the same day or over several days)

- early specialization in a sport or activity
- improper equipment or footwear
- prior injury
- adolescent growth spurt (can cause growth plate and muscle-tendon injuries)
- absence or alterations of the menstrual cycle leading to stress fractures of the bone
- poor training or sports technique

The right combination of training, rest, and recovery can give the athlete the best chance of optimizing physical performance and preventing injury.

Sleep to Enhance Performance

Sleep plays an essential role in the human body's growth, physiological recovery, and rejuvenation, independent of the individual's age or circumstances. Due to our busy lifestyles, sleep deprivation (lack of sleep) is becoming increasingly prevalent in both adults and children. In individuals who do not get adequate sleep, there is a dramatic increase in the prevalence of obesity.[3] Children with shorter sleep duration have a 58 percent higher risk of being overweight or obese. In children, there was a 9 percent reduction in obesity for every hour of increased sleep.[4] Research studies show that children between five and twelve years old need ten to twelve hours of sleep per night. The longer the duration of the child and adolescent's sleep the greater the general health benefit.[5] For example, in a study of 2,300 US children aged three to twelve years, it was determined that those children who slept more than eleven hours per night had better overall fitness, improved health, and less risk of obesity at a five-year follow-up time period.[6]

Why does sleep affect health?

The poor health picture in those children and adolescents who are sleep deprived is due to changes in the body's endocrine function. A lack of sleep has been linked to increased sympathetic activity, elevated cortisol and adrenalin levels, decreased leptin and growth hormone, impaired glucose tolerance, increased insulin resistance, increased basal metabolic rate, and increased depression rates.[7] Those endocrine processes are essential for the developing athlete both mentally and physically.

Proper sleep by itself has been shown to affect athletic performance in a positive way. For example, a study of college basketball players found an increase in shooting accuracy with increased sleep. The study showed that college players who increased their sleep to more than ten hours per night increased their free-throw accuracy by 9 percent and their three-point accuracy by 9.2 percent.[8] That increase in basketball shooting percentage could make an average player good and a good player great. From a team perspective, that increased accuracy could lead to a significant increase in wins.

In both Major League Baseball (MLB) and the National Football League (NFL), studies show that a lack of sleep will decrease the athlete's opportunity to make a team following being drafted. In MLB, the player's chance of making the team increased from 38 percent to 57 percent when they were more rested. In the NFL, the better-rested players made the team 56 percent of the time, while their less-rested counterparts made the team 39 percent of the time.[9]

The lack of sleep can also negatively impact injuries related to exercise training and competition. Athletes have up to a 90 percent increased risk of injuries when sleep deprived. It is believed that the lack of sleep impairs the body's ability to regenerate damaged tissue and replenish depleted energy stores.[10] This lack of proper healing leads to excessive body breakdown that is not repaired for the next training or competition.

As the individual ages, the sleep needs change. From puberty to approximately twenty-six years of age, individuals need 9 to 9¼ hours of sleep. Interestingly, as the required hours of sleep change, the time of day that sleep is needed also changes. Teenager's brains are biologically programed to fall asleep around 2 or 3 A.M. and wake up around 10 or 11 A.M. This is counter to our academic culture, in which most middle and high schools start between 7 and 8 A.M. Because of this, approximately 80 percent of teens do not get enough sleep per night. Unfortunately, due to extracurricular activities, the school schedule will most likely not change.

The critical stages of a good night's sleep

Sleep can be divided into two components, non-REM and REM (rapid eye movement). There are four stages to non-REM sleep, which occurs first in the sleep cycle. During the fourth stage of non-REM sleep, there is also the secretion of human growth hormone, which stimulates muscle development and tissue repair. This phase of sleep is critical for the development of the competitive athlete. During this final phase of non-REM sleep, blood pressure drops, respiration slows, and blood flow to muscle decreases. After the fourth phase of non-REM sleep, the body enters REM sleep.

During REM sleep, the brain blood flow, respiration, pulse rate, blood pressure, and body temperature increases. All the day's activities and experiences are solidified into memory. Cognitive memory (frontal cortex) and muscle memory (motor cortex) are enhanced and developed during REM sleep. Skills and movement tasks that were rehearsed or practiced during the day become reinforced and learned to a higher level. During this phase of rest, skill and athleticism are developing to a higher level.[11]

The whole cycle of sleep, from non-REM to REM, lasts approximately ninety minutes. During a typical night's sleep, there are approximately four to five cycles.

Ten key factors to obtaining a good night's sleep

1. Avoid caffeine after 2 P.M. Caffeine can be in the body for approximately six hours.
2. Avoid juices, sodas, caffeinated beverages, alcohol, and high-sugar desserts.
3. Avoid high-fat foods, spicy foods, meats high in protein, processed foods, or MSG before bed.
4. Foods such as nuts, seeds, turkey, peanut or almond butter, cereals or oats, crackers, vegetables, bananas, eggs, and milk will help you sleep due to tryptophan and/or melatonin.
5. Limit the use of electronics (TVs, computers, iPads, phones, and tablet readers) an hour before bed. Melatonin (hormone that

facilitates sleep) release is blocked from the blue-spectrum light emitted from screens.

6. The bedroom should be dark, quiet, and cool (65–67 degrees).
7. The pillow should not be too flexible. If you fold it in half and it does not instantly open, it is time for a new pillow.
8. Journal or write down thoughts or worries from the day prior to bedtime. Writing down these ideas will help clear the mind prior to sleep.
9. Meditation and deep breathing can help relax the body. Breathe in to a count of four, hold the breath for a count of two, and blow out the air for a count of four.
10. Maintain a consistent sleep schedule. Go to sleep and wake up at the same times every day.

Napping to enhance sports performance

A twenty- or ninety-minute nap during the day can be used to refresh individuals not getting enough sleep at night. Do not do anything between those times. Naps under twenty minutes keep the individual in non-REM sleep. If the nap is between twenty and ninety minutes, the individual may wake up during REM sleep, which will lead to feeling malaise and fatigued upon wakening.

Before a game or competition, this type of nap could increase skill performance by 16 percent versus those who are sleep deprived. It is typical to see professional athletes take naps during the day to enhance performance during games.[12]

There are the six steps to a perfect nap:

1. A daily nap is especially needed if the individual is getting less than 7½ to 9¼ hours of nightly sleep, depending on age.
2. Choose either twenty minutes or ninety minutes for the nap.
3. Consider earplugs and an eye mask to eliminate noise or light.
4. Keep the room cool, between 65 and 68 degrees Fahrenheit.
5. Lie down for the nap; avoid sitting up.
6. Clear your mind with deep breathing as described above.[13]

In conclusion, from childhood to adolescence to adulthood, there is a clear association between sleep duration and health. For the training athlete, in order to make the desired physical adaptations, it is essential to optimize sleep using the above-mentioned strategies and principles.

References

1 Sarah Mottram and Mark Comerford, "A New Perspective on Risk Assessment," *Physical Therapy in Sport* 9 no. 1 (2008): 40–51.

2 Hans Selye, *The Physiology and Pathology of Exposure to Stress* (Montreal: Medical Publisher, 1950); B. A. Spiering et al., "Resistance Exercise Biology: Manipulation of Resistance Exercise Programme Variables Determines the Responses of Cellular and Molecular Signaling Pathways," *Sports Medicine* 38 no. 7 (2008): 527–540.

3 Janna Flint et al., "Association between inadequate sleep and insulin resistance in obese children," *Journal of Pediatrics* 150 (2007): 364–369.

4 Ibid.

5 W. Stewart Agras et al., "Risk Factors for Childhood Overweight: A Prospective Study from Birth to 9.5 Years," *Journal of Pediatrics* 145 (2004): 20–25; Emily K. Snell, Emma K. Adam, and Greg J. Duncan, "Sleep and the Body Mass Index and Overweight Status of Children and Adolescents," *Child Development* 78 (2007): 309–323.

6 Snell, Adam, Duncan. "Sleep and the Body Mass Index."

7 Karine Spiegel et al., "Leptin Levels Are Dependent on Sleep Duration: Relationships with Sympathovagal Balance, Carbohydrate Regulation, Cortisol, and Thyrotropin," *Journal of Clinical Endocrinology and Metabolism* 89 (2004): 5762–5771; Shahrad Taheri et al., "Short Sleep Duration Is Associated with Reduced Leptin, Elevated Ghrelin, and Increased Body Mass Index," *PLoS Medicine* 1 no. 3 (Dec 2004).

8 Cheri D. Mah et al., "The Effects of Sleep Extension on the Athletic Performance of Collegiate Basketball Players," *Sleep* 34 no. 7 (2011): 943–950.

9 Ben Potenziano et al., "Sleepiness As a Predictor of Players Longevity within Major League Baseball," *Sleep* 35 Abs 0801:A273 (2012); S. L. Rogers SL et al., "Sleepiness As a Predictor of Draft Value in the National Football League," *Sleep* 35 Abs 0211:A76 (2011).

10 Richard Budgett, "Fatigue and Underperformance in Athletes: The Overtraining Syndrome," *British Journal of Sports Medicine* 32 no. 2 (1998): 107–110.

11 James B. Maas JB and Haley A. Davis, *Sleep to Win! Secrets to Unlocking your Athletic Excellence in Every Sport* (Bloomington, IN: AuthorHouse, 2013).

12 Ibid.

13 Ibid.

Conclusion

Based on the scientific evidence, it is clear that all youth and adolescents should be involved in a healthy, active lifestyle. Exercise and training for the young athlete is the missing link to reaching optimal athleticism, improving sports performance, and minimizing the risk of injury. Train 2 Play Sports' objective is to create durability and ability in the young athlete. The information discussed in this book lays the basic framework on scientific training principles that will be used in future writings to help the athlete optimize physical development. These writings will then be used to build exercise programs specific to the individual athlete's needs based on the biomechanics of his or her sport. Any exercise that is given to an athlete should have a specific reason to "why" it is given. Remembering the SAID principle, specific adaptation to imposed demand, the body will adapt and respond specifically to the training. The more specific the training to the athlete's sport the more crossover and opportunity for sports enhancement and injury prevention.

Please go to train2playsports.com and sign up for our insiders club to receive the latest training news and be notified of new releases of future books.

62003507R00062

Made in the USA
Middletown, DE
17 January 2018